LOOK AT WI
MAR...

MW00427500

"No one speaks to teens about sex more powerfully and practically than Jacob Aranza does in *Making a Love That Lasts*. Listen up, moms and dads—this is the book you should give your daughters and sons to keep them on the path to purity."

BILL MCCARTNEY
FOUNDER OF PROMISE KEEPERS

"This is the single best basic book clearly dealing with sexual temptation and relationships for the young that I have ever read. Simply, funny, and wholly practical, Jacob points out a sure and wise path for being and staying morally clean, and building a love and marriage that lasts a lifetime."

WINKEY PRATNEY
INTERNATIONAL YOUTH EVANGELIST AND
AUTHOR OF *YOUTH AFLAME*

"Never before have I read a book that so uniquely exposes the lies about sex and relationships among youth. From Jacob's years of ministering to young people across the nation, he has successfully combined real stories and experiences with godly principles in *Making a Love That Lasts*."

JOHN BLUE
PROFESSIONAL HOCKEY PLAYER–BUFFALO SABERS

Making a Love That Lasts

How to Find Love without Settling for Sex

JACOB ARANZA

Servant Publications
Ann Arbor, Michigan

Vine Books is an imprint of Servant Publications especially designed to serve evangelical Christians.

Although the stories in this book are true, names have been changed to protect the privacy of those involved.

Published by Servant Publications
P.O. Box 8617
Ann Arbor, Michigan 48107

Cover design: PAZ Design Group, Salem, Oregon

   97 98 99 00 10 9 8 7 6 5 4 3 2

Printed in the United States of America
ISBN 1-56955-019-0

Library of Congress Cataloging-in-Publication Data

Aranza, Jacob
      Making a love that lasts : how to find love without settling for sex / Jacob Aranza.
         p.   cm.
      Includes bibliographical references.
      ISBN 1-56955-019-0
      1. Love—Religious aspects—Christianity.   2. Sex—Religious aspects—Christianity.   3. Sexual ethics for teenagers.   I. Title.
BV4639.A64 1996
241'.66—dc20   96-43157
                                                               CIP

This book is dedicated to
Jacob Jr. and Christian,
Natalie and Thomas,
William and Elizabeth,
Zack and Andrew,
Brittany and Buggy,
Cameron, Aldon, and Mamie,
Haley and Asley,
Mathew and Lauren,
And to all our friends and family.
God in you is the light of the world.

To a world filled with darkness
God always sends his light.
May you walk in purity and allow
His light to shine to the next generation.

Contents

Acknowledgments

The author would like to express
sincere thanks to
Walter Walker,
Heidi Hess,
and special thanks to
Bert Ghezzi
for believing all things
are possible. You were right!

Foreword

NO ONE HAS TO TELL YOU how desperate our generation is for answers. Never have there been more voices with advice on the issues of sex than today, and yet fewer people than ever know the true meaning of love, sex, and intimacy. Ten years ago, I heard Jacob Aranza for the first time. He has been uniquely raised up from a family of immorality, adversity, divorce, and dysfunction as one of God's miracles. His life is an expression of God's awesome ability to reach anyone, anywhere, and restore that person to his design. For the past twenty years Jacob has been proclaiming a message of hope and purity to the most neglected and abused generation in American history. He has spoken face-to-face with more than two million students around the world, calling them to a higher standard. In addition to the countless others, my children and their friends have been touched by Jacob's life and message. What you are about to read is not theory but principles that have transformed the life of the author and the lives of students all across the world. Quite often, books addressing sex speak only to those who have waited... this book is filled with hope for those whose shattered sexual lives are in ruins, and who believe there is no new beginning. God offers a clean heart for a new start... and that new start can be yours.

Josh McDowell

Preface

LARRY WALTERS HAD A SECRET DREAM. Since he was thirteen years old, he had dreamed of being the pilot of an enormous airliner. But Larry realized early that, for many reasons, his dream would not come true.

He did have a back-up plan, however. One bright day, with the help of his girlfriend and a few neighbors, Larry strapped himself into an aluminum lawn chair equipped with a CB radio, a parachute, and a BB gun. Attached to the chair were forty weather balloons, all filled to capacity with helium.

With his neighbors and friends manning ropes attached to the chair, Larry was reeled out like a kite high above the neighborhood. For the would-be pilot who was determined to fly, whatever it took, it was a thrilling experience.

All went well until the ground crew got a little careless, and the ropes got away from them. Quickly, Larry began to gain altitude until he had a panoramic view of the city of Los Angeles. A pilot from an airliner flying over the city radioed the tower to report a flying lawn chair at sixteen thousand feet. Larry began to send out a Mayday on his CB. At that altitude he was beginning to get a little numb and tingly, so he decided it was about time to start taking out some of the balloons with his BB gun.

Naturally, he began to lose altitude, but it wasn't necessarily a controlled descent; there's no way to steer a lawn chair! When he was almost all the way down, his flying chair became entangled in electrical wires. Larry's chair came to rest, dangling from the wires, about five feet off the ground. He unbuckled his seat belt and fell to the ground, unharmed.

Every teenager dreams of one day beginning a love relationship that will last for a lifetime. Many are as desperate to find that true love as Larry was to pilot his own aircraft. They usually start out on what they expect to be a safe but exciting adventure to make their dream become a reality. Unfortunately, like Larry's chair, things can get way out of control, and these teens wind up making a dangerous descent. They set in motion a chain of events and emotions that in time become unmanageable.

There is a way to pursue a lasting relationship without becoming an emotional casualty yourself. If you follow the plan, you too can see your dreams of love for a lifetime come true.

Introduction

IT'S HARD TO CHANGE COURSE after your life gets started off hard into one direction. But that's exactly what happened to me. I started getting off track way back in the third grade.

The defining moment and turning point of my young little life came when I tied into a guy named Charlie Garnett. In the long run it didn't turn out to be one of my better days. Charlie was the biggest third grader anyone had ever seen. He was an imposing figure and he had the strangest hair, kind of wavy. It went in all directions, but you can be sure that no one ever kidded him about it.

Charlie didn't have a lot of other things going for him, so he became the class bully and set a personal goal of having a major impact on every guy in the class. By "major impact" I don't mean Charlie was trying to set a stellar example for us. If you weren't careful to stay out of his way, sooner or later his big fist was going to make a personal impact on your face.

As the skinniest kid in the school, I was pretty careful to stay clear of Charlie. But all that ended one Friday after show-and-tell.

There was a shopping center in downtown Houston where for the price of a bag of popcorn and an extra nickel, you could buy a goldfish. Along with this goldfish I got a little bowl and some blue rocks to put in the bottom. I was really pumped up about displaying my goldfish at show-and-tell.

I'm not sure what it was about that goldfish that set off Charlie Garnett. Nevertheless, he determined that I was going to be his Victim of the Day. After school he followed me home. He kept pushing me, trying to get me to fight. Every push splashed a little more water out of the bowl. I was only about a block and a half from home, but I knew that even though I was a faster runner, I probably couldn't get away carrying my books and a goldfish bowl too. It was either me or the goldfish.

I took seriously my responsibilities as a third-grade goldfish owner. I put the bowl down and turned to Charlie and said, "I don't wanna fight, but if you're determined, let's go for it." That's all he was waiting for. Charlie started swinging.

Charlie was big and chunky. I was skinny and fast. I knew I had to do something quickly or this situation could get really ugly. When Charlie swung, I ducked, and his body weight caused him to lunge right past me. Taking advantage of the opportunity, I quickly got him in a head lock. It was like a flea hanging on to a mad elephant by the head. Eventually, he fell to the ground, and I jumped on him and pinned his shoulders with my knees. Charlie hollered and screamed and threatened to kill me, but I never would let him up. Finally, he agreed to quit fighting if I got off. Of course, I should have known better.

Back in those days it was really cool to wear platform shoes. The taller your platforms, the cooler you were—and I happened to be *very* cool. One thing about those shoes was that after a while the heels would wear down and expose the little nails. And walking on the concrete only sharpened them more. When I started to get up Charlie grabbed my leg and tried to pull me down. Trying to catch my balance, I swung my foot around and, with all my weight behind it, I planted the heel of that platform shoe squarely in the center of Charlie Garnett's forehead. While bleeding Charlie was rolling on the ground screaming, I scooped up my goldfish and ran home.

The next morning, the first person that met me at school said, "Man, I heard you and Charlie Garnett really got it on yesterday."

"Well, I guess so."

The next person said, "Man, I heard you whipped Charlie Garnett yesterday!"

"Well, I guess I did," I responded.

By lunch time everyone was talking about how I had gotten sick and tired of Charlie Garnett, and had just whipped him. Of course, whenever Charlie walked by everyone noticed the big bandage on his forehead.

By the end of the day people were saying, "Do you know what Jacob Aranza does to people he doesn't like? He's got these shoes with nails he has sharpened sticking out the heels, and he'll use 'em to stomp on your face and pound his mark into your forehead."

Before this, no one had paid much attention to me, but overnight I had gained a reputation. I never had been one of those kids all the teachers wanted to have in their class to start with, but after my encounter with Charlie Garnett, things took a decided turn for the worse. For the next five years of my life, I wound up trying to live up to my new reputation and to the worst expectations people had of me.

A lot of kids today are living up to the expectations people have for them. The problem is that nobody expects too much. Do you know what kids say when they are asked about their greatest desire? The number one response is that they want to live in a happy family. But three out of four kids in school today come from families that have split apart. Many of them have come from three generations of broken homes on both sides of their family. It's like one of those big pileups on the freeway. One car gets out of control, the next one hits him, then the next car, then the next car, and so on. A lot of kids come from families that are not just a wreck, they are a multi-generational pileup. Why should they expect their life to be any different?

It's getting to the point where a single person who remains a virgin until his or her wedding night is about as rare as a moon rock. Surveys show that as many as eight out of ten couples are sexually involved before their wedding night. With so many doing it, it comes to be expected of you. What makes you think you'll be able to be any different?

Over a million unmarried teenagers get pregnant every year. And what happens to these girls and their babies? Studies show that 500,000 of them have abortions. The other 500,000 give their babies up for adoption, or decide to keep them. Eighty percent of pregnant teenage girls drop out of school. Seventy percent of the unwed mothers go on welfare. Sixty percent of the teenage mothers who marry because of the pregnancy will divorce in five years. A lot of kids have given up hope of ever escaping this pattern. They'll become another statistic, just like everyone expects.

I understand what it feels like to see your life rolling right down the tracks of other people's worst expectations of you. I know that feeling of having no reason to expect that you're going to be any different from all the rest of the people around you. My mother and father raised me in the black and the Mexican ghettoes of Houston, Texas. I had four sisters who had all gotten pregnant or married by the ages of thirteen, fourteen, fifteen, and sixteen.

I had a lot going against me. Nevertheless, when I was fifteen years old I took a sharp turn that put hope back into my life. Today I have a beautiful wife and wonderful marriage that has lasted fifteen years and four sons who are the joy of my life. No one expected Jacob Aranza to do or be anything in life. I was a bad statistic waiting to happen.

I've got great news for you. You don't have to live down to other people's worst expectations. You don't have to become a statistic. There's hope that the best things in life can still come your way. Believe me, if it can happen to me, it can happen to anyone—you too!

1 ▼ Legends of Hot Love

Have you ever felt the sting of finding out that someone you really trusted was regularly lying to you? Just because someone is your friend doesn't mean that that person won't lie to you. Lying has become such an accepted practice, many people do it without even thinking that it's wrong. James Patterson and Peter Kim, authors of *The Day America Told the Truth*, found in their surveys that 91 percent of Americans lie regularly, by their own report. Eighty-six percent said they lied to their parents regularly, and 75 percent reported that they lie regularly to their friends.[1]

There are a lot of reasons why people lie: to cover up something they did or did not do, to get along with everyone, to look cool, to get something they want, or to simply mask their own fears and insecurities. All of these can be powerful temptations to lie, especially to people for whom telling the truth is no big deal.

Those are only a few of many reasons *why* people lie so much, but do you know what people lie *about* more than anything else? You probably guessed it: SEX! People will almost never tell you the truth about their sex lives and *absolutely never* tell you the whole truth. Even your friends lie about it. Most of you know people who have never done anything sexually, yet they brag about all that they have done. You also know people who have done a whole lot and swear they haven't done anything.

The reason why people lie so much about having (or not having) sex is that there is a long list of personal needs that people are trying to fulfill with sex, if not by actually doing it, by simply talking about it. Having sex is not just a matter of physical pleasure; there are a lot of other issues involved. People want to be accepted, they want to look cool, they want to attract attention, they want to be intriguing, and they want to be loved. People desperately want to measure up. If a guy admits that he's never had sex, he may be afraid that someone will think him to be less of a man. Sexual temptation is a mixed brew of boiling hormones, insecurities, fears, peer pressure, and intimidation.

I've had the privilege of speaking to over two million students on five different continents. I have also had the chance to counsel with thousands of students about their first sexual encounters. I've asked these young people how they really felt about these encounters. If I have discovered anything through all those conversations, it is this: *What kids say about sex when they're really honest with me is almost never what they have told their friends.* They aren't trying to impress me and they know I'm a safe person to open up with.

Besides, you know how hard it is to tell a single lie, because you always have to tell a second one to uphold the first one. As eighteenth-century American painter Washington Allston once observed, "Nothing is rarer than a solitary lie; for lies breed like toads; you cannot tell one but out it comes with a hundred young ones on its back."

Surveys show that friends are the number one source of a teen's information about sex. You can get a lot of good help from your friends when it comes to your schoolwork, your jump shot, and the best places to shop for clothes. In most cases, however, listening too closely to your friend's advice about sex is definitely a bad idea. The same kind of internal pressures and conflicts that cause people to lie about sex will also cause them to give advice that is way off target.

And, hey, bad advice is especially easy to come by because it gives people a chance to grind their axe about their parents, to whine about their "ex," or to justify the mess they are making of their own life. Whether people are getting too involved physically or lying about it in one way or another, they go through an intense internal battle with their own moral conscience. It's a lot easier to lie about premarital sex than it is to actually do it.

There's one lesson about life you need to learn very early. If someone wants to give you advice, you'd better find out what's motivating his or her words. Is this person trying to sell you something or to get you to do something? Whenever someone wants to give you advice about sex, you've got to ask yourself, *What is behind these opinions and why am I being told about them?* Are there unresolved issues in this person's life that influence the way he or she thinks?

Sex is a subject that is so often talked about and so consistently misrepresented that it will always create quite a few legends. There are a lot of myths about sex that exist among teenagers and older singles. Here are the three hottest:

Myth Number One: *Sex is the ultimate fulfillment, and if you haven't done it, you are really missing out.* If that were true, then the happiest people on earth would be the ones who have the most sex. However, ultimate loneliness and emptiness is found in the heart of a prostitute. Believe me, I know; if you'd grown up in my neighborhood, you'd know it too. According to the myth, she and her customers should be happy all the time, and prostitution should be the most fulfilling livelihood of all—a career of enjoying what is supposed to be the ultimate fulfillment, and getting paid for it too! The truth is that people who look for fulfillment in sex are terribly disappointed, and they become the least fulfilled.

Look at the lives of your friends who are most sexually active. Have you ever heard people sitting around talking about the first time they had sex?

"We made love, and it was great!"

That's almost always a lie. When they really get honest, do you know what guys who have had premarital sex say to me about the first time? "Is that all...? I just thought it would be more than it was. It was over so quickly. We both felt so terrible about what we were doing that it really wasn't fun... especially after it was all over."

You know what most girls say when they get honest? "He was all over me and I really didn't want to.... I feel now like part of me is gone that I will never be able to get back again. I sure hope he doesn't tell anyone. I always wanted my first to be so special—not like this."

There's only one first time, but don't think that if someone has lost their virginity then there's nothing else to lose. You always give away a part of yourself each time you have sex. The myth: sex is the thing that ultimately fulfills. The truth: sex outside of marriage causes you to lose a little more of yourself each time. Eventually, you wind up feeling completely empty. Sex outside of lifetime commitment doesn't make you feel as if someone has added something to you. It makes you feel they have taken something very valuable away.

Myth Number Two: *Sex before marriage and sex after marriage are the same.* You won't have to look very far to find someone who will advise you that what makes sex acceptable or not acceptable is simply love. "It's okay if you really love each other." Ever heard that? What this person is really saying is that it is feelings of love—not the lifelong marriage covenant—that distinguishes "right sex" from "wrong sex."

As I said before, people will give you bad advice about sex. But what really gets bizarre is when they begin to talk about their definition of true love, especially when they assume that a free ticket to sex comes with it. Most of the time "love" means no more than Johnny, the guy on the commercial, telling a girl, "I luv U, man," when all he really wants is her Bud Light (or a babe light).

Sex before marriage and sex after marriage (with your spouse, that is) are two entirely different things. A girl who was a junior in a high school in Anaheim, California, told me that. Years ago I was speaking in her school, which is located right across from Disneyland. Pattie's dad had asked me to talk to her because her life had taken a number of turns for the worse. I shared a few things with Pattie that I hoped would challenge her thinking. She looked at me, then said sincerely, "Jacob, I appreciate your talking to the kids in my school and what you've done for them, but I'm basically a party animal now, and I know it. My life is a mess, but I really don't want to change. If I ever do, though, I'll let you know."

About six months later I heard again from her dad. Pattie had gotten involved with her church youth group, and she had committed her life to Christ. A year later I found out that she was dating a guy who was going to be a minister. Two years later I found out that they were engaged and were about to be married. When we met again about six months after their marriage, Pattie called me aside, insisting that we had to talk. Here's what she said:

There is something I have to tell you that you have to tell kids you speak to in schools. Jacob, sex before marriage and sex after marriage are two entirely different things. Before marriage there was guilt, the fear of getting pregnant or of my parents finding out. What if I get some disease? Will he break up with me now that I've given in?

Since we've been married, sex has been so beautiful. We had the blessings of God and the blessings of my mom and dad. Even the minister looked at us as we left the church and said, "Have a good time!" Sex before marriage and sex after marriage are two entirely different things. You have to tell kids that!

Sex in a loving marriage is one of the greatest and most fulfilling things on earth. Sex outside of marriage is spiritually, emotionally, and mentally toxic for everyone involved. Don't let anyone tell you differently. Don't believe the lie!

Myth Number Three: *You can build a relationship on sex.* At the very end of the movie *Speed* (1994), Jack (Keanu Reeves) says to Annie (Sandra Bullock), "I've heard that relationships based on intense experiences never work."

Annie replies, "OK, we'll just have to base it on sex."

Then they go for each other's tonsils, the music starts, and the assumption is they live happily ever after.

WRONG! It was a pretty good movie up to that point, but they blew it on the last scene. Keanu Reeves and Sandra Bullock!— they're so cool. How many people would love to be like them? Here's the myth being perpetuated by the media.

Why do so many couples attempt to build relationships on sex? The answer is not too difficult. For guys, it's easier to get undressed physically than it is to open up emotionally. On the other hand, many girls give in to sexual advances because they are looking for emotional intimacy, and are later sorry. Girls most often look for commitment, while guys most often look for contact.

Psychologist Rollo May said, "There is so much use of the body as a substitute for psychological intimacy. It's much easier to jump in bed with someone than it is to share your fears and anxieties. Because the body is used as kind of a buffer, the intimacy gets short-circuited and never becomes real intimacy."[2]

Have you ever wondered why the most sexually desirable and liberated people on earth (i.e., entertainment celebrities) seem to have the most difficulty with lasting relationships? When two stars get married, few people will bet a dime against a dollar that it will last more than a few years. Sexual liberation has left them almost completely dysfunctional with regard to lasting relationships. Lasting relationships, even marital relationships, are not built on sex. In fact, whenever two people begin to use sex as the primary means of cementing their relationship together, the relationship always begins to deteriorate.

Haven't we all heard stories about people who have gone together for quite a while, had sex, and within weeks their relationship ended? It shows that you can't build a relationship on sex, but you sure can *end* one! One girl, after giving in and then getting dumped, said it like this: "I loved him, I loved him, I loved him—then I let him, and I lost him."

Many guys have said the same thing to me.

Jacob, I didn't want to be involved in sex. Both my girlfriend and I were pressured by all our friends who kept asking, "Hey, are you two doing it?" And so finally we did. And instead of gaining something, we lost something. We lost respect for each other. We could hardly look each other in the eye. We couldn't look our parents in the eye either. We lost each other.

There's a story in the Bible that exemplifies what bad advice about premarital sex does to a relationship. Absalom, the son of

Abigail and King David (of Goliath fame), had a beautiful sister whose name was Tamar. Amnon was the son of David by another woman. The Bible says that Amnon loved his stepsister Tamar.

And Amnon was so frustrated because of his sister Tamar that he made himself ill, for she was a virgin, and it seemed hard to Amnon to do anything to her. But Amnon had a friend whose name was Jonadab...and Jonadab was a very shrewd [deceptive] man. And he said to him, "O son of the king, why are you so depressed morning after morning? Will you not tell me?"

Then Amnon said to him, "I am in love with Tamar, the sister of my [step-] brother Absalom."

Jonadab then said to him, "Lie down on your bed and pretend to be ill; when your father comes to see you, say to him, 'Please let my sister Tamar come and give me some food to eat, and let her prepare the food in my sight, that I may see it and eat from her hand.'"

So Tamar went to her brother Amnon's house, and he was lying down. And she took dough, kneaded it, made cakes in his sight, and baked the cakes. And she took the pan and dished them out before him, but he refused to eat. And Amnon said, "Have everyone go out from me...." Then Amnon said to Tamar, "Bring the food into the bedroom, that I may eat from your hand."   2 SAMUEL 13:2-6, 8-10

If nothing else, this is an example of how bad advice about love can come from a good friend. But there's another lesson here as well. Look at what happens next.

When she brought them to him to eat, he took hold of her and said to her, "Come, lie [have sex] with me, my sister."

But she answered him, "No, my brother, do not violate me, for such a thing is not done in Israel; do not do this disgraceful thing! As for me, where could I get rid of my reproach? And as for you, you will be like one of the fools in Israel. Now therefore, please speak to the king, for he will not withhold me from you [as a wife]."

However, he would not listen to her; since he was stronger than she, he violated [raped] her and lay with her.

2 SAMUEL 13:11-15

Amnon had proclaimed that his love for Tamar was so great that he couldn't stand the sexual frustration anymore of not having her. Ever heard that one before? The next verses are what is most interesting and most revealing:

Then Amnon hated her with a very great hatred; for the hatred with which he hated her was greater than the love with which he had loved her.

And Amnon said to her, "Get up, go away!"

But she said to him, "No, because this wrong in sending me away is greater than the other that you have done to me!" Yet he would not listen to her.   2 SAMUEL 13:15-16

Did Amnon ever really love Tamar, as he said he did? Perhaps not even Amnon himself knew. Maybe he just said he loved her, but all he ever actually wanted was just to get her in bed and claim her as a trophy. In either case, all his love (or his pretense of love) vanished as soon as they had sex. Mark it down, people. Premarital sex won't strengthen your relationship; it'll only tear it apart.

Myth Busters

One of the most prolific myth busters of all time was Socrates. He lived in the fifth century B.C. and was the greatest of the Greek philosophers. Socrates' "claim to fame" was that he simply loved the truth and sought for wisdom.

Socrates was sure that no wise man would deliberately choose what was bad for him in the long run, although he did admit that through their ignorance men often chose an evil that appeared to be good at the time. Socrates likened himself to a gadfly who went about stinging the Athenians with his endless questions, hoping to awaken in them the search for wisdom and a more noble life. Eventually he ran amuck of the powers-that-be in Athenian society by insinuating that the myths to which they gave credence without any good reason were not only keeping them from true wisdom but were also morally corrupting the young people. His simple probing questions revealed their underlying motives for believing myths. But people don't give up their myths easily. Socrates was sentenced to death and was forced to drink a cup of poison hemlock.

I won't kid you; if you dare to be different, it will probably cost you. But then again, if you just go with the crowd, it'll cost you even more. At some point you've got to start making decisions based on what is right and what is best for you, not on what pleases everyone else. It takes a lot of courage to have an honest heart, one that is willing to hear the truth even when it goes against the current (politically correct) myths of morality. That's what it takes to get free from the traps of sexual myths.

It takes courage—and better information. Keep reading if you want more of both.

2 ▼ Good Needs, Bad Deeds

Everybody needs to be loved. Everyone wants to experience acceptance and approval from the people who matter. It's the way God made us. The big question is: How should we fill those needs?

It's scary to think back on the things I did to gain acceptance and approval. I was raised in the black ghetto of Houston called Sunnyside. It was, to say the least, a rough neighborhood. Some of the members of the notorious Black Panthers were from Sunnyside.

I used to walk down the street listening to my boom-box singing, "Say it loud, I'm black and I'm proud." I thought my skin was a little bright, but it never occurred to me that I wasn't black. Everyone else knew it, though, and I never totally fit in. Soon after I realized why I was being treated differently, we moved—from the black ghetto to the Mexican ghetto.

My parents separated when I was nine. Eventually, I moved into a house that adjoined a bar. I became a member of a small street gang called the Devil's Children. We did a lot of crazy things, and the main reason, at least for me, was peer pressure. The Devil's Children was not like your basic Boy Scout troop. In order to get initiated they told me I had to go beat up this guy who was a lot bigger than I was. I was scared. But more than being afraid of the fight, I was afraid of not being accepted. I just wanted to be a part.

I took drugs from the time I was nine until I was almost fifteen. Soon after I started, I began selling them, too. I got started in drugs by sniffing gasoline. Now I never sat down and said, "I just think I'll sniff some gasoline today." It was all my friends saying, "Hey, man, this is cool; this is really rad; you've gotta do it, man." And so I did. We all did—that is, until a kid in the neighborhood died doing it. Just about everything I did, especially the bad stuff, was because of peer pressure. I so much wanted to fit in and be accepted. Kids don't usually join gangs because they just want to be bad. Street gangs are a type of support group for those who want to feel like they belong. My sister was a member of a motorcycle gang, *The Bandidos*. They were my idols, and I wanted to be just like them.

If someone had said, "Let's go jump off the tallest building in Houston," I guess I would have been right there with them. I was such easy prey because I had such a tremendous need to feel loved, to feel special, and to feel accepted.

How much of a target are you? How susceptible are you to temptation? How much are you influenced by the opinions or the pressure from your friends? Do you have the ability to make your own decisions and then stand firm, even if you have to stand alone? The answer to these questions depends a lot on the degree to which particular needs have been met in your private life. You may not have grown up in the same kind of neighborhoods as I did, but we all have the same needs. The important thing is where we look to fulfill those needs.

Building a Strong "Love" Foundation

It is important to have a strong foundation of acceptance, approval, and affection in your life. Our Creator meant for each of us to find acceptance, approval, and affection in a family—a place where people love you for who you are, no strings attached.

Of course, no family is perfect. I understand what it's like not to have a stable family life. My mother married a couple of times, and one of my stepfathers had been married seven times. Since my mother divorced my dad, he has been married three more times. The woman he married after my mom had been married three times previously. The woman he married after her had also been married three times. They divorced too, and my father has now married and divorced his fourth wife. I don't have a family tree; I've got a family *bush*. I have no idea who all I am related to. Don't laugh. I may be related to you!

I know what it's like when family members can't get along. Michelle and I had a lot to be nervous about when our families got together for our wedding rehearsal dinner. My dad and his third wife sat on one side, and my mom and her second husband sat on the other. You could feel the tension in the air. They took turns offering toasts to Michelle and me, wishing us happiness— and that we would never be so unfortunate as to have to live with someone like the person sitting across the table! We got through it OK, but I was afraid it would turn into one of those brawls like the ones you sometimes see on "Geraldo."

I had always wanted to be loved, accepted, and approved of because I never had those needs met at home. I was always looking for something to fill the void. But the things I did to fill that hole only made me feel more empty.

Maybe you know about this empty feeling that comes from not finding the love you need at home. *Jacob,* you might be saying, *you don't understand the kind of family I came from! You don't know all the stuff that goes on at home.* But even if your family isn't perfect, there are still good places for you to find the love and support you need.

Ask God to lead you to people who can show you the right kind of love. Maybe it will be a Christian family in your neighborhood. Or maybe you can build closer ties to your church youth group. The church is supposed to be an instrument of God's unconditional love. It may not be a perfect instrument—everyone makes mistakes from time to time. But by finding a church "home," you will get the moral support you need to make good choices. You will begin to build a "love foundation" for yourself that will make you strong inside, and help you to make good choices for how you live your life.

If you get the love, acceptance, and affection you need from the right places—such as your family and Christian friends—you will be able to say "no" to all kinds of temptations. If there are weak spots in your "love foundation," Satan will use those weaknesses against you. He will exploit your God-given needs for love and acceptance, and tempt you to try to meet those needs in the wrong way.

Temptation is Satan's promise (mixed with our own desires) to provide for any unmet needs we might have—in ways that God never intended. Think about this: Every sin against God is simply an attempt to get for ourselves, in our own way and in our own timing, the things that God himself very much wants us to have. These temptations might seem like a good thing at the time. But it's always a bad deal because Satan never delivers on his promises. When we throw out God's plan for our own agenda, the fulfillment of our needs never works out the way we had hoped.

The "Big Three" Needs Everybody Has

In his wisdom, God put the need for acceptance, approval, and affection deep inside each of us, in the private places of our hearts. These needs are a normal and healthy part of being human. But the desires themselves can be so strong that some people will do almost anything to fill them! Let's take a brief look at each one, as well as good ways and dangerous ways to meet each of those needs.

The Need for *Acceptance*

Everyone, without exception, has an essential need to be accepted. We all want to feel included as a part of a group. But what people are actually looking for is something deeper than just being "in with the crowd." The desire of every person's heart is to have secure, enduring relationships that are based on trust and mutual acceptance. It is one of the most driving forces in an individual's life.

A sense of acceptance is fundamental to our emotional stability. When we don't get acceptance from others, it's hard to feel good about ourselves. It doesn't take long for us to begin to believe we are *unacceptable* and that we'll never have friends. The first place where we should learn acceptance is at home. Unfortunately, kids learn some memorable lessons about rejection there too. Only one out of every four kids in elementary school today have both of their biological parents living in their home. That means that there are a lot of unmet needs in the lives of many kids at the most important time of their lives.

Then there's school itself. Unless you've spent your entire time in school hanging out in the broom closet, you know firsthand how ruthless kids can be, especially the most popular kids. Acceptance is usually based on dress, looks, personality, humor, daring, or athletic ability. Stop and look around sometime and notice how hard everyone is working to be accepted. It's a performance scale that's very hard for some people to measure up to. Consequently, some kids give up and rebel against the "in crowd" and against everything and everybody who sets standards for them. They hate principals, police, parents, and preppies because they resent all their requirements for acceptance.

A few years ago I was speaking in an open marketplace in England. Tall Mexicans with a Texas accent are not that common in England, and so I quickly drew a crowd. There was one guy who really caught my attention. It could have been because his hair was six different colors, he wore tight leopard-skin pants, and there were pins stuck all through his face. When I had finished speaking, he walked up to me and said, "Hey, man, what's wrong with you?"

You're asking what is wrong with ME? I thought to myself.

Most kids like this guy have experienced a lot of rejection long before they get into punk rock. At some point, they gave up trying to be accepted and determined that they just didn't care. Some kids resort to extreme measures to demonstrate that they don't care about the standards anymore. Not only have they quit trying to measure up to people's criteria in order to gain acceptance, they delight in deliberately violating the rules because it shocks people, causing them to reject the rebels even more. This rejection gives these teens another peer group of their own—the "rejects."

What they are looking for is unconditional love and for people just to accept them for who they are. In a way I admire people who decide to be their own person. However, in rejecting all the rules (including God's rules), they ignore the warning signs and get on the wrong ramp going in the wrong direction. Consequently, they're cruising into a head-on disaster.

While some people rebel against the status quo, others are desperate for it at any price. People who long for those secure relationships are tempted to perform, compromise, or pay any price in order to be accepted. In both cases, the need for acceptance causes lots of pressure. The fear of rejection can drive people to do some crazy things. I got a letter from a girl named Sharon whose life was being controlled by her fear of rejection.

During my years in high school, I was like the rest of my friends who were interested in doing whatever was fun and exciting. I knew there was a God, but I did my best not to think about him. When I was about fifteen, I met this guy. He was several years older than me and seemed much more mature than the other high school guys. I thought he was really good-looking, and so we started dating. After a few dates he wanted to have sex, but I turned his offer down because I hardly knew him.

As time went on I began to get scared that he would find another girlfriend. The fear of losing him was more than I could take, not because I loved him, but because I loved the attention and affection that he gave me. Many of my friends were sleeping with their boyfriends, and a few were on the pill. I started feeling like I was missing out on all the fun and excitement. It was because of these two reasons that I decided to try it.

Sex seemed fun at first, but I never dreamed it would turn out so badly. Over the next year our relationship got worse and worse. Mike had a horrible temper, and I was always afraid of him. It was like we hated each other. Several times I broke up with him, but we always ended up together again. All he had to do was put his arms around me, and I would go back to him. The physical attachment was so strong. I guess it's like the Bible says, that when two people are joined together, they become one flesh. I took a lot of physical and emotional abuse from him. What is so strange is that I never loved him! He was just an experiment that made me miserable, one that I couldn't give up.

Sharon was in a relationship that had turned destructive, one she couldn't get out of because her fear had her trapped, not by love but by her need for acceptance and her fear of rejection.

The conventional wisdom is that girls never want to have sex, but they give in order to get love. Guys, on the other hand, have no internal restraint; all they want is sex. Those stereotypes are often inaccurate. A friend of mine wrote and shared with me about the sexual opportunities that had been presented to him when he was single.

During my high school and college years there were only three girls whom I dated steadily. There were a couple of instances in which the girl I was dating was ready and willing to have sex. I knew it was the wrong thing at the wrong time. On both occasions I stopped what was about to happen. In one case I jumped up and ran out.

I realize that I should have never let myself get into those situations. Sometimes I even wonder how I was able to say no to the opportunity. But I understand looking back on it now that what I was really "into" was the relationship. Being that girl's boyfriend made me feel accepted and good about myself. What made me turn down the opportunity for sex was (1) the fact that I was feeling the pressure of tremendous guilt, and (2) I was afraid that if we had sex, the girl would start feeling guilty and break up with me. As much as I wanted to go all the way, I was afraid of losing the relationship.

Eventually those relationships faded, and years later I met the girl that I wound up marrying. We were both virgins on our wedding night. We've been married fifteen years now, and I'm so glad we both waited for each other.

Guys have just as great a need for acceptance as do girls. We all need the acceptance of people around us. But listen, don't let the devil take your need for acceptance and use it as a means of controlling and destroying your life.

The Need for *Approval*

We all want approval from people who care about us. Approval has been one of the greatest slave drivers of all time. It will take a person captive and never let him go until he feels as though he is finally a success in the eyes of others.

I remember talking to a college basketball coach who told me about one of his players named Bill. When Bill was in high school, he had all the qualities of a great basketball player: the skill, the height, the speed, and the jumping ability. Yet Bill never played up to his potential. Bill's family never showed much interest in his basketball, never encouraged him, and never came to see him play. It appeared to the coach and to Bill also that they just didn't care. In his senior year, there was a change in Bill's family, and they began attending the games. He became the top scorer and rebounder on his team. The approval of his family gave Bill the confidence he needed. If someone tells you that they don't care what anyone thinks, don't believe it. We all care. We need the acceptance and approval of others because acceptance and approval help us establish our own self-worth and self-esteem. We're all at some stage in this process.

Approving of ourselves has to do with our self-esteem and our self-worth. In their survey, James Patterson and Peter Kim asked people what they would do for $10 million. Twenty-three percent responded that they would be a prostitute for a week.[1]

How much are you worth in your own eyes? How do you develop a higher self-worth?

The place where it begins is at home, particularly with your father. For better or worse, your father's ability to express unconditional approval of you is foundational for your emotional well-being. I don't need to tell you that many, many fathers fail their kids, even pretty decent fathers. Your dad's father may have failed him, too. If your home life has left you with an unmet need for approval, you may find yourself expressing bitterness or rebellion. You may shop around for another source of approval. One reason I'm working so hard to tell kids about sex is so their unmet need for approval doesn't automatically propel them into the embrace of the nearest warm body. If you know your home life has left you emotionally deprived, it's important to realize that this affects your decisions. You won't regret seeking help from your church or from a counselor or other trusted adult.

Just because a father is absent from the home doesn't mean he can't or doesn't provide that emotional foundation for his kids. Unfortunately, many kids feel that no matter how hard they try, they can never measure up to their father's performance standards in order to win his approval. Sometimes the unmet need for approval turns into rebellion and bitterness. It so saddens me every time I hear of a kid being molested by parents or relatives. These kids are left feeling so shamed and cheapened that self-esteem and self-worth are hard to come by. Some kids from broken homes miss out on the positive affirmation they need and are even made to feel responsible for their parents' divorce.

This unmet need for approval can be like a trap for you. You need to be alert for enticements that the devil may try to lure you with. Guys or girls who are themselves "on the prowl for sex" can immediately spot a person with a low self-worth and an unmet need for approval. Like predators zeroing in for the kill, they'll promise to provide the approval you need. If you want it bad enough, you'll fall into the trap and they'll get what they want from you too.

How valuable are you? Try calculating your net worth with this in mind: God loves you so much, even with ALL of your failures and shortcomings, that he gave his only Son to be tortured on a cross for you. When you realize that he esteems you so highly, that he considers you to be of such great value, you'll think twice before you give yourself away to gain someone else's approval.

The Need for *Affection*

I remember all my life looking for affection. The reason again was because I didn't find it at home. All of us want someone to be affectionate with us—preferably someone good-looking. The truth is that people with a desperate need for affection often wind up looking for love in all the wrong places. If, as they say, love is blind, people looking for love because of an unmet need in their lives are not only blind but also deaf and dumb. They throw all reason, morality, and respectability to the wind because they *gotta be loved by somebody.*

When I was growing up, my favorite snacks were the pickles and lemons we used to get at Mr. Pat's grocery store. The more sour they were, the better. Later I found out a possible reason for my preference: apparently, people often have a craving for lemons because of a vitamin deficiency. Our amazing internal biological systems can identify a vitamin deficiency which, in turn, triggers a craving for a food needed to remedy that lack in our bodies.

Studies show that girls who have healthy relationships with their fathers are less likely to get involved with premarital sex. A father's pure love and affection provides some special emotional "nutrient" for a daughter. When it's not there, an internal warning light goes off, but the alert is not easy for a girl to interpret. Often she doesn't realize until a long pattern of relationships with guys has been established that she is not looking for a boyfriend but a father figure. She is looking for someone who will meet the needs her father never met.

The signal of a girl's deficiency of fatherly love can be displayed in many ways. In any case, it is an alert to a father, uncles, grandfathers, and sometimes even big brothers that there is a serious father-love deficiency.

A friend of mine tells his teenage daughters, "When you're looking for a husband, look for a guy that loves you as much as I do." Girls who know what healthy love from their dad feels like are not as likely to fall head over heels or feel obligated to a guy simply because he says, "I love you."

It's not just girls I'm talking to, of course. Believe me, I know how tough it is for guys who grow up without a dad at home. What begins as a *sadness* over the absence of a father's love often turns into an angry *madness*. Sometimes guys even take out their frustrations on their mother, which leads to more and more conflicts with the woman who is desperately trying to be a mom, a dad, and a provider too. She begins to "lay down the law," but the guy's resentment over being dominated by a woman grows and grows. Unfortunately, some of these young men grow up feeling their ticket to manhood is gained by dominating or sexually conquering as many women as they can, seeking to rule over those who once ruled over them. You've seen the unhealthy pattern in our culture. It's a vicious cycle, a mutual struggle for dominion which doesn't solve anything. The emptiness is still there, the unmet need for approval and affection.

Sometimes the emptiness doesn't result in such violence, but sexual attraction is mistakenly confused with an unmet need for affection. Shelly was a girl who looked no different from any of her friends. Her cute figure and outgoing personality got her lots of immediate attention from the guys. She was what the guys called "a babe." The one thing that did set Shelly apart was that she *had to have* a boyfriend at all times. Ever since she could remember, she had always had one. Her mom and dad had divorced when she was two years old. Living with her mom hadn't always been the best, but they usually got along. Her dad tried to stay in touch, but his new wife, along with his job, preoccupied most of his time. Shelly admired her girl friends who didn't seem to need a guy like she did. *Why can't I be as happy as they are without a guy in my life?* she often asked herself. In a large part because of the absence of her father, Shelly had a great need for affection that she just couldn't get filled.

Some of you reading this book have been going with someone almost all your life. And if you weren't going with somebody, you were looking for someone to go with. If you were going with somebody, you had two or three people hanging on the line in case you broke up; that way you could hook up with someone else as quickly as possible. In short, you've tried to find your identity, security, and self-worth in being hooked up with someone.

The real issue for all of us, male or female, is this: Where do we really find our significance, and in whom do we really find fulfillment?

Bisexuality and Homosexuality:
The Ultimate in Sexual Confusion

After a high school assembly in Wichita, Kansas, a young attractive girl walked up to me after everyone else had left the gym. "Jacob," she said, "I have to tell you something I have never told anyone before." Looking around to be sure no one was in sight she whispered, "I'm gay."

"Who told you that you were gay?" I whispered back.

"No one; I just know that I am."

"Have you ever been involved sexually with another girl?"

"No," she replied.

"Well, then how do you know you're gay?"

She thought for a few seconds about how to respond and finally said, "There's a girl I like here at school. Whenever she goes out with a guy, it makes me angry. I want her friendship just for myself."

I asked about her parents. They both live at home, and she even said that they were pretty close.

"When was the last time they told you that they loved you?" I asked.

"Well..." she began, but paused as if she was searching through her past, trying to find a way to explain, "we don't say things like that in my family."

"When was the last time your mother hugged you?"

"We don't do things like that either," she confessed.

I was amazed, and continued to probe. "Has you mother *ever* hugged you and told you she loved you?"

"Not that I can remember," was her sad answer.

"Sweetheart," I said, "I don't think you're gay; you're just looking for some motherly love in a time when you're also going through a hormonal explosion." Her story was a familiar one. I've heard many such stories from hundreds of young people whom I have counseled over the years. Their stories have three characteristics in common that cause great sexual confusion in teens, which in turn has led some to conclude they are homosexual or bisexual. These three factors are:

1. No strong father figure present in the home. What happens to a boy who is raised by his mother and never bonds with a father or a father figure? At puberty the hormones kick into gear, and he longs for an outlet for his sexual desires. At the same time he is yearning psychologically and emotionally for the love of a father. The longing for a father figure can sometimes result in inappropriate sexual behavior in both young men and young women, including promiscuity, bisexuality, and homosexuality.

2. Childhood molestation or abuse. The memories of childhood homosexual encounters can follow a person into adulthood, and damage both the victim's sense of self-worth and his or her sexual identity. Victims of these types of crimes often have deep-seated roots of anger and fear that cause additional confusion.

3. Parental abandonment or neglect. Some kids resort to inappropriate sexual behavior as an attention-getting device, to get the adult attention they crave. For this reason, bisexuality has become a cultural trend among kids today, much as biracial dating was prevalent in their parents' generation. (The difference is that homosexual and bisexual relationships are wrong according to God, whereas arguments against biracial dating are often based largely on social prejudice.)

Pop culture icons openly flaunt their sexual "preferences" for shock value. But think about it. Twenty years from now, after the shock wears off, will these celebrities still be idolized? Or will they be drowned out as the stars of the next generation take their place?

Ask your parents who their "teen idols" were. You'll probably hear names like Elvis Presley or the Beatles. By today's standards their music is pretty tame. But years ago parents were shocked by these icons. The music was a reflection of the Sexual Revolution that had exploded and shaken our culture's values at the roots. We discovered too late that "free love" was neither free nor love. And we continue to pay the price.

Homosexuality and bisexuality are products of a culture that no longer has defined sexual roles. Many couples have abandoned the belief that protecting, preparing, and providing for their children is their primary responsibility in life. This value has been replaced by the quest for power, pleasure, and possessions. This was not the case twenty years ago, and in most cases your parents were not raised this way. Unfortunately for you, these changes in our society make developing a sexual identity more difficult now than ever before.

Difficult, but not impossible. It's up to you: Who are you going to look up to in life? And what can they teach you that one day you will want to pass on to your *own* children?

Same Old Thing

People who fall into sexual temptations do so because they desperately want love, affection, and intimacy. I have already made this point, but I want to emphasize it: *God wants them to have these things as well!* But the way these people go about having those needs fulfilled is outside of God's plan for their lives. Unfortunately, that mistake does not fulfill the needs, but even compounds the problems.

There's nothing new about the schemes of the devil. Jesus was tempted in the same way we are. That's why it says in the Bible, "We don't have a priest who is out of touch with our reality. He's been through weakness and testing, experienced it all—all but the sin" (Hebrews 4:15, THE MESSAGE).

After his baptism when the Holy Spirit descended upon Jesus in the form of a dove, he was led by the Spirit into the wilderness to be tempted by the devil. Jesus was taken to the pinnacle of the temple by Satan and propositioned: "If you are the Son throw yourself down," the idea being that God would save him, and that, of course, would do a lot for his popularity and acceptance as the Jews' Messiah. On another occasion Satan showed him the kingdoms of the world and offered them to Jesus if he would fall down and worship Satan.

What was Satan's strategy? He was promising Jesus what he was already destined to receive—to rule over all creation. The temptation was to get in the wrong way what God the Father intended all along to give him. In the same way each of us is tempted by Satan. It's the "short cut" to getting that for which we are not yet ready.

The same thing happened to Adam and Eve. In the beginning God placed two trees in the Garden of Eden, the Tree of Life and the Tree of the Knowledge of Good and Evil. You've probably heard this story before, but let me give you a quick review. God had said to Adam and Eve that they could eat from any tree, except from the one in the center of the Garden of Eden, the Tree of the Knowledge of Good and Evil. Up to that point there was no knowledge of sin and selfishness.

Satan came to Eve in the form of a serpent to tempt her by saying that God was really trying to keep something good from them. And so she took the bait, ate the fruit, and learned the knowledge of evil. When you trace back through the long chain of the cause and effect of evil in this world, that act was the prime mover, the first domino that was tipped over.

Adam and Eve were expelled from the garden so that they would not be able to "take also from the tree of life, and eat, and live forever." Adam and Eve sinned against God trying to obtain what God wanted all along to give them, and in the process, they lost everything.

How does all this apply to you? God's plan and desire is that the need for love, approval, and acceptance in your life be fully met. But don't let your emotional needs turn into emotional bondage. God has a better plan if you'll do things his way. Remember—he's the Author and Creator of life and love. His guidelines give us the opportunity to experience these at their fullest.

3 ▼ Threatening Sex

Dear Jacob,

You came to my school a few weeks ago. I only wish you had come earlier. Recently, a few of my girlfriends and I had a sleep-over. They were all talking about their "first time." It finally got around to me, and they said, "What was your first time like?" I was the only virgin in the room, the only one who had never had a first time.

When I told them that, they started questioning me, "Isn't there anyone you like?"

Finally I said to one of the girls, "Well, I think your brother is kind of cute."

"Then write him a note and tell him you want to be with him," she said.

Not because I wanted to but because of the pressure of my friends, I wrote him a note. He wrote a note back to me at school the next day: "If you meant what you said in the letter, come home with my sister after school on Friday."

By Friday every one of my friends knew all about it, and I felt there was no way out. I walked to his house with his sister. When we got in, I laid down my books, and he motioned for me to come upstairs. I looked at his sister and then walked upstairs. When I got to the top he said, "Are you sure you want to do this?"

Jacob, in my heart I was saying no, but, instead, I just nodded my head, yes. We walked inside his bedroom, and he locked the door behind me. He turned on some music, began to kiss me, and said, "Are you sure you want to do this?"

Jacob, in my heart I wanted to say NO, but I just nodded my head yes. We got undressed and got in bed. We had just begun to have sex when a knock came at the door. His boss was downstairs waiting for him to go to work. He jumped up and began to throw on his clothes. He pointed and said, "The bathroom is over there."

As soon as he left I got up, locked the door, went into the bathroom, and got in the shower. I thought, Well, my friends should be proud of me. It's over, I've done it. I'm not a virgin anymore.

But, Jacob, I never thought about the terrible feeling of guilt that would cover my heart. All I could think about was him walking out that door saying, "I'll see you later."

I can't help but feel that when he walked out of that door part of me walked out with him.

From Temptation to Intimidation

That was probably the most honest letter I've ever received from a teenager. You see, a lot of people are trapped by temptation. Satan holds out a carrot, something that they have come to want so badly that they are willing to exchange something of much greater value for it. Sometimes they are tempted by the false promise of an unmet need being fulfilled. On the other hand, a great many people are sexually trapped, not by temptation but by intimidation. They get involved sexually because they are manipulated or bullied into it. The Bible has a lot to say about those who are intimidated as well as about those who do the intimidating.

The Book of Revelation was written by the Apostle John. The resurrected Christ appeared to him while he was in prison on the island of Patmos. Jesus instructed John to send messages to the seven churches in Asia Minor. To the church in Thyatira he sent this message:

> The Son of God, who has eyes like a flame of fire and feet like burnished bronze, says this: "I know your deeds, and your love and faith and service and perseverance, and that your deeds of late are greater than at first. But I have this against you, that you tolerate the woman Jezebel, who calls herself a prophetess, and she teaches and leads my bond-servants astray, so that they commit acts of immorality."
>
> REVELATION 2:18-20, NAB

There's a lot of symbolism in the Book of Revelation, and the name of the woman used here was probably symbolic as well. The Old Testament Jezebel was the wife of Ahab, one of the kings of ancient Israel. She was the daughter of a foreign king whom Ahab had married to establish a political alliance. She was a seductress and a Baal-worshiper (idol-worshiper). As a zealous pagan, she intimidated and manipulated Ahab into committing all sorts of immorality. Jezebel did away with the prophets of the Lord and introduced the worship of Baal with its cult prostitutes, child sacrifices, and elaborate sex orgies. Jezebel is forever a symbol of someone who dominates and intimidates people into committing acts of spiritual and sexual immorality, the very thing that happened to Greg:

Jacob,

I remained a virgin until I got out of high school and began working as a chef at a restaurant. Word got around, and before I knew it, a race began between the waitresses to see who could take my virginity! Since they came after me, not wanting any commitment from me, I just thought of sex as a recreation—like sports. Once I had had it, I became hooked and got into a lot of sexual relationships just for the fun of it.

There are a lot of people around today, both male and female, who have the spirit of a Jezebel; they seduce, dominate, and control people by intimidation and lead them to "commit acts of immorality." I've heard people say that they *agreed* to have sex together, and, therefore, they equally bore the responsibility for it. But in many cases the truth was that one of them was determined to have sex and coerced the other one into it.

Let me give a very serious and sobering piece of advice. In fact, you may wish after reading it that you had never heard this. So if you don't want to know the hard truth, you'd better drop this book right now!

Still with us, huh? This next story gives a very sobering piece of advice.

Later Ahab asked God to forgive him. He changed and received mercy from God (1 Kings 21:29), but the anger and the judgment of God weighed in heavily against Jezebel. God decreed that she would die and that the dogs would eat her, which in fact did happen (2 Kings 9:10, 33-37). Of course, you can't say that that level of judgment applies to every person who, like Jezebel, causes a weaker person to stumble sexually. Yeah, but listen to what Jesus himself said to his disciples:

> It is inevitable that stumbling blocks should come, but woe to him through whom they come! It would be better for him if a millstone were hung around his neck and he were thrown into the sea, than that he should cause one of these little ones to stumble.   LUKE 17:1-2, THE MESSAGE

A Christian friend of mine wrote this account about a relationship he had in high school. Here's part of what he wrote:

> I was a junior in high school and Susan was a sophomore when we started dating. She was cute, naive, and a little "spacy." I was certainly the more dominant person emotionally, intellectually, and even spiritually. I had already become a Christian. As time went on, though, our relationship was less and less spiritual and more and more physical. I wanted to break up because I didn't really have a strong emotional attachment to her. But I had gotten addicted to the physical stuff, and it was just too tempting.

We never went all the way, but one night we almost did. I had always felt terribly convicted by the Holy Spirit about all the touching and making out. But when I left her house that night, the feeling was very different. Driving home I had such a vivid sense that God was angry about what I was doing. I was exploiting my dominance over a weaker person in such a way that, if it continued, it would rob her of her virginity. I had such a penetrating sense of God's displeasure that night. You might say literally that it scared the hell out of me! I asked for God's forgiveness and broke that relationship off immediately. She was really hurt, but I was about to hurt both of us in a much more long-lasting way.

Maybe you are someone who has been intimidated and exploited. Maybe you are the one who has taken advantage of other people. Perhaps, you've been in the kind of relationships where people just use each other for their own desires. In any case, please keep reading because before you finish this book I want to show you how you can be made clean and pure again, how you can have a fresh start and be *just as if you had never sinned*. But first, the two points I want you to see right now are:

1. *Many people stumble sexually because of the intimidation of others.* You don't want to let that happen to you because not only are you hurt, but each of us is responsible for his or her own decisions. You can say, "The devil made me do it," but, in the end, there are no excuses. You are the one who has to live with your choices and accept responsibility for them.

2. Some people think like the lyrics of Sheryl Crow's song—"All I Wanna Do Is Have Some Fun." But Jesus Christ who sits in heaven doesn't always see it that way. Listen to me—both guys and girls—you absolutely do not want to be someone who causes others, particularly weaker ones, to stumble. It's a heavy responsibility, and you *do not* want that millstone hangin' around your neck. As the Bible says, he who has eyes of fire knows what you are doing, and you don't want to look like a Jezebel in his eyes.

Toxic Relationships

Sharon was the girl whose letter you read in the previous chapter. She had given in to the continual pressure from Mike to have sex because of her fear of rejection. But soon afterward it began to turn into a toxic relationship. Through intimidation and even physical abuse, Sharon was bound by a controlling influence. Sharon was so dominated that she couldn't get out of the relationship. That's a sad situation but one I have seen many times.

Are you in an abusive relationship?

There are many forms of abuse that signal that you are in a bad relationship. Here are just a few:

- Your partner intentionally embarrasses you in front of others.
- Your partner manipulates you to try to get his or her own way.
- Your partner constantly cuts you down or demands that you change.
- Your partner intentionally hits or hurts you.

- Your partner has frequent temper tantrums or emotional out-bursts.
- Your partner's jealousy or anger seems to control your actions.

All of these things can happen either to guys or to girls. I've seen so many singles unable to get out of abusive relationships because they *thought* they were in love. Love is unselfish and, therefore, seeks to give. Lust always takes. People who have "fall-en in lust" (as opposed to "fallen in love") are, more than any-thing else, in love with themselves. Girls and guys, listen to what God has to say about real love: "Love is patient [it can always wait], love is kind [never abusive], *and* is not jealous [not posses-sive];...does not seek its own [not self-centered]; and is not pro-voked [quick tempered]" (1 Corinthians 13:4-5, NAB, additions mine).

Are you being poisoned by a toxic relationship?

People who are driven by lust are continual "takers" in relation-ships. Sometimes that means they use people for a brief time, then discard them. For others, it's not enough to be using some-one; they want to possess that person. People stuck in control-ling, possessive relationships, especially girls, are often bound by fear, guilt—or both. In extreme cases they are kept in tow by threats such as "If you leave I'll hurt you and anyone you go out with." Sometimes they are manipulated by guilt: "I'll kill myself if you leave!"

Unbelievably, some teenagers actually do attempt suicide over a lost love. Sometimes it's for revenge, sometimes out of sorrow, but most of the time it's a form of guilt manipulation to keep their girlfriend or boyfriend from leaving.

Committing suicide over a dating relationship? Most of you probably think, *Oh, PU-LEASE! Get real!* But you have to understand how powerful the need for acceptance, approval, and affection can be, and understand how empty some people are. They are desperately struggling with all sorts of unresolved issues and unmet needs in their lives. The only answer seems to be to hang on to another person who usually is just as messed up. There is nothing sadder than two people, both of them major "takers," each trying to squeeze something out of a relationship to try to fill the huge void inside. They usually wind up hurting, if not destroying, each other. Many of you have seen firsthand examples of two people who are both bad for each other, but they are so mutually dependent, neither can let go.

Sometimes an abusive person will swing between being very nice, kind, and gentle to being abusive and out of control. You keep thinking that if the good side could overcome the bad side then this would be a great person. Don't wait for that! And don't fool yourself into thinking that you're going to change the abuser. Don't allow that person's promises to change to become another means of controlling you. Get out of the relationship, or you may face a life that becomes a sad cycle of emotional or physical abuse!

Some people, out of their own insecurities, become obsessed with a certain person. Sometimes both partners have the same kind of obsessive need for each other. Psychologists call this a *codependent relationship*. Don't get this kind of attachment confused with true love. Codependent people can become so possessive that they refuse to allow the other person to have any kind of independent life. They are so jealous that they wind up smothering each other emotionally. Codependency is when you feel you can never be happy alone. You must find happiness in someone else (meaning that your happiness is not dependent on your own actions but the actions of someone else).

I have often seen teenagers who wanted to break up with their boyfriend or girlfriend but stayed in the relationship because they were afraid to hurt the other person's feelings. This may be commendable, but it definitely is not love. Charity dating—that is, going out with someone just because you are afraid of hurting them—is cruel. Not only do you give the other person a false idea of your interest, but you are keeping him or her from finding the one that is really a right match. We all know that "breaking up is hard to do." But breaking up or saying "no" to someone is not the end of the world. Don't ever stay in a relationship out of fear, guilt, or pity. Anything that is not built on love will eventually fall apart in a way more painful than just "breaking up."

Let's review the basics: Satan always looks for the chink in your armor, tempting you in the area of your most painful unmet needs. If that doesn't work, he uses people and circumstances to intimidate you at the point of your greatest fears. His purpose is to rob you of your own virtue and self-worth, to sidetrack you from God's plan for your life, and ultimately to put you into bondage. He will do anything to try to keep you from finding your identity in God through a relationship with Jesus Christ.

You can mark this down: The greatest, most fulfilling and enduring relationships occur when two people are mature enough to find, in God and in their family, their own sense of identity and security. Their own inner needs are met so that they can enter a relationship as a giver, not a taker or even a domineering possessor. By that definition of maturity, a lot of adults have grown old but have never grown up.

4 ▼ The Grim Reaper of Great Relationships

What kind of marriage do you hope to have someday? Do you see a white picket fence with 2.5 kids playing in the yard? Maybe you dream of you and your mate both being in positions of power, each with your own Lexus. Some people may see themselves sailing off into the sunset with their spouse, in search of adventure in a foreign country. All of these are great dreams, but understand this: They'll turn into nightmares without a solid relationship between you and your lifelong mate.

The greatest marriage relationships are those in which both are secure in each other's love, commitment, and faithfulness. Both are in the relationship to *give* love, not just *get* it! There is a likeness of mind and a common purpose. For both, the relationship comes first, and they protect it from the things that would weaken it. They refuse to live angry even for a single day. They both are ready to sacrifice, to put the other's needs and wishes first. Separation is never an option. They are joined until death. If they win or lose, they do it together. They are inseparable. They are one.

Have you ever noticed that girls spend most of their lives dreaming about their wedding day, while all the guys have been dreaming about is the honeymoon? For a single man the thought of sex any time, any day is almost too much to comprehend. He thinks marriage means sex in the morning, at night, and a quicky on lunch break. But surveys show the average married couple has sex three times a week.

"Not me," you say. "I'm gonna do it three times a day!"

That's great. When you get married, go for it. But you have to understand that there's a lot more to marriage than sex. If the average couple has sex three times a week, that's about two to three hours at the most. What happens the rest of the time? One survey asked thirty thousand women about how they chose their husbands. Most of them said they had chosen their mates based on sex appeal, but 80 percent said that if they had it to do over again, they would choose a husband based upon his ability to communicate. In another survey of 730 therapists and marriage counselors, 85 percent said that the number-one thing their clients complain about is the lack of communication.

People who marry primarily for sex rarely stay together very long. On the other hand, to have a good relationship, the kind that fulfills God's purpose for you, you've gotta have a lot of good sex too. When God created Eve and presented her to Adam, he didn't just say, "Now I want you to talk, share your hearts, work together, and be friends." Of course not. They were standing there naked, looking at each other, and God said, "Go for it! Have sex, have babies, and do it a lot. Your job is to populate the earth!" Adam's previous job had been naming animals. This was quite a promotion! Adam said about his new wife, "This is now bone of my bones, and flesh of my flesh" (Genesis 2:23). The next verses in the Bible say this:

For this cause a man shall leave his father and his mother, and shall cleave to his wife; and they shall become one flesh.

GENESIS 2:24

A man's relationship with his wife is different from any other relationship. Regular, exciting, creative, romantic, passionate sex is what makes the difference. Sex in marriage is what gives people physical, emotional, and spiritual oneness. Sex takes an already great relationship to another level and causes two people to be one.

Sex Is Beautiful by Design

In the movie *The Gods Must Be Crazy*, someone flying over the plains of Africa threw out an empty Coke bottle. It was found by a man who took it and showed it to his tribal leaders. No one had ever seen such a thing. It was obviously designed by some intelligent being. So they concluded that it was a gift sent to them by the gods, but they had no idea what it was for. They tried using it for every imaginable purpose. Before long they were all fighting over the bottle. Finally, they threw it over the cliff, concluding that the gods must have been crazy to send them such a thing.

When people don't understand something's purpose, they usually misuse or abuse it. Many people abuse sex because they don't understand its true purpose. From the beginning, sex was given as a special gift for the purpose of bringing oneness, procreation, and pleasure—to be used only in marriage. Two different bodies, each with different personalities, strengths, and weaknesses, come together in a one-time, lifelong covenant of oneness. The clear understanding of God's purpose is seen in the results of sex. A child is produced, but it's neither the man nor the woman alone who is responsible for the child. The kid looks a little like mom and a little like dad—in one person, the expression of them both.

Whether or not sex produces a child, sex is much more than a physical act of pleasure or reproduction. It is a giving of oneself emotionally and spiritually. Just as both the man and the woman contribute to the creation of a child, in the act of sex they each contribute some of their own soul. God designed this act of love to produce a lasting bond—in marriage. When two people have sex outside of marriage (misusing God's original intention or purpose), that bond is broken. This is part of the reason why after each different sexual relationship, people feel that part of themselves has been given away. They are misusing a gift God designed for a special purpose—to bind together a husband and wife.

There is a second type of bond that two married people create between them—a bond of emotional intimacy. Just as sex outside of marriage goes against the "design" God created, building this kind of emotional intimacy outside of marriage can be just as painful. I call it "playing married." We'll take a look at this a little later, but first let's take a look at what a *healthy* dating relationship is like.

Finding "Mr." or "Miss" Right Doesn't Have to Hurt

What's your favorite sport? Tennis, basketball, volleyball? Whatever it is, you've probably learned that the more you practice something, the better you get at it. "Practice makes perfect," they say. But what if you are practicing something that you don't want to be good at—like breaking your own heart time and time again? The truth is, the relationship "habits" you establish now will be with you the rest of your life. So you want to be sure you "practice" the right ones!

In *Call It Love or Call It Quits,* Tim Timmons and Charlie Hedges describe the four stages of healthy dating relationships as "hoping," "scoping," "coping," and "roping."[1] I first heard Tim use these terms on a TBS program fifteen years ago. Since that time I have adapted these stages to help many teens and singles develop good dating patterns. Let's take a look at each one:

1. Hoping: This is the "pre-dating" stage when you look across the room and see some cute girl (or guy) and say to yourself, "Wow! I'd like to get to know that person better." At this stage you experience an attraction that makes you want to be around that other person. You also wonder whether that person might be interested in *you.* There is no real emotional or physical involvement at this stage.

2. Scoping: At this stage a real friendship develops. "Dating" may take the form of going to the movies or out with friends. You see what the other person is like in different situations, how he or she treats other people. You may spend time with each other's families, or together at group social events. "What does she look like without makeup?" "What does he like to do with his spare time?" You get to know each other's likes and dislikes, and come to understand a little more about each other's values and goals. There should be little emotional or physical involvement at this stage.

3. Coping: As the relationship progresses, both people begin to ask themselves some important questions.

First, consider your own situation. Are you ready to be able to make a lifelong commitment to another person? Those who marry too young—before they have had an opportunity to fully discover their own identities, goals, and needs—are in danger of becoming another divorce statistic.

Second, consider the other person. "Could I really live with this person for the rest of my life?" "Can I deal with all his (or her) strengths and weaknesses?" Josh McDowell said it best when he observed: "Don't marry someone you can live with—marry someone you can't live without."

It's also important to take a close look at your partner's *family.* Do you enjoy being around them? Can you imagine being a part of their family? Do you and your partner share similar goals and values?

It is always wise to seek the advice of married people with a proven "marital track record." They can help you to uncover any potential problem areas, and to help you to decide whether to take your relationship to the next level. It is at the next level—marriage—that the deepest level of emotional and physical bonding should occur.

4. Roping: You have met someone, checked him (or her) out, and decided that you want to commit to this person for the rest of your life. In marriage you are free to bond at every level—mentally, emotionally, and physically.

Unless you understand the developmental stages of relationships, you may be tempted to go from "hope" to "rope" in a short period of time. Or, you may be tempted to get involved before you are mentally or emotionally ready to make such a commitment.

"Playing Married" and "Practicing Divorce"

Sometimes young couples get carried away and don't take the time to go through all the stages of their relationship. They become emotionally attached very quickly, before they know enough about each other to tell whether there is a basis for a long-lasting relationship. I call that "playing married." When you begin to "play married," your whole world begins to revolve around the person you are with. Everything and everyone else fades into the background. But what happens when your relationship is over? You guessed it—you begin to "practice divorce." One reason divorce rates are so high is that by the time people get married they have had a lot of practice breaking off relationships, rather than working things through when things get tough.

Why is it that teens get caught up in this cycle of unhealthy emotional attachments in their dating relationships? Part of it is human nature, the longing for closeness.

After dating for awhile, a guy or girl (perhaps both) begins to think, "Could this be the one?" They imagine themselves as husband and wife, and, for awhile, it gives them a real thrill. But as time goes on, the thrill isn't what it was in the beginning. So sexual fantasies enter into the picture, along with the temptation to take things "to the next level." The problem with "playing married," mentally and emotionally, is that it's only a matter of time before there is an overwhelming temptation to act it out physically.

If you're a Christian, then your heart belongs to God, and you really don't have the right to give it away until he shows you the one he has purposed for you to marry. The first time I met Michelle I felt we were meant for each other. I couldn't stop thinking about her. But I knew that my heart as well as my body belonged to God, and I really had to guard my mind until I knew for sure and she said, "Yes." In other words, don't allow yourself to fantasize or "play married" until you actually are.

The cycle of "playing married" is fun at first, kind of like a honeymoon. But just like playing anything, the time comes when the game is over. When these "marriages" hit a rough spot and the couple breaks up, the emotional devastation is similar to what couples go through when a marriage ends. And once you have been mentally, emotionally, and physically involved, what you experience is not a game, but actual separation.

At the beginning of this section I said that if you practice anything, you'll probably get pretty good at it. But is divorce something you want to be good at? That's why it's important to learn how to build healthy dating relationships now—so you don't get in the habit of suffering the pain of broken relationships.

Sex Is Like Masking Tape...

How? Let's look at an example. Say a girl begins high school as a fourteen-year-old (who, unfortunately, looks like she's twenty). Everything in the media has reinforced the idea that she needs to dress, think, and act much older than she really is. Before long she's dating an older guy. Within six months they're all over each other, and eight months into the relationship they've gone all the way. You've seen similar scenarios before, and you know that many couples don't even wait that long!

Let's suppose that by the end of her freshman year she has broken up with this guy and has another boyfriend. By the time she graduates from high school she has had two or three relationships like this. (Again, that's a conservative estimate.) By the time she's graduated from college, this girl may have had five relationships like this.

Now her wedding day arrives. It's time for her to walk down the aisle. What is the difference between this commitment and all the others? Is it only flowers, a nice dress, and a piece of paper? Unfortunately, the only difference for many people is that the expectations are a lot higher. However, she's already been through five divorces. So when things get difficult in the actual marriage, what's she going to do? She's probably going to say, "I'm outta here!" That's the response at which she is most practiced.

Sex is the part of marriage that cements two people into oneness. You might think of sex as a kind of emotional "masking tape." Why? Stick a piece of real masking tape on a surface and then remove it. Stick it to another surface and remove it again. Do this several more times. You'll notice that on each new surface the sticking power is less. People are like tape; the more they get stuck together with a person sexually and then detached, the less sticking power they have. The purpose of sex in marriage is to provide the oneness that sticks them together permanently.

The Bible says:

There's more to sex than mere skin on skin. Sex is as much spiritual mystery as physical fact. As written in Scripture, "The two become one." 1 CORINTHIANS 6:16, THE MESSAGE

If, in fact, you become one with every person with whom you have sex, by the time you get married a lot of people are going to be pretty diluted. Is it any wonder that as the average number of premarital sexual partners has increased, so has the divorce rate? When you've become one flesh with one other, two others, or twenty others, you've lost the sticking power of a sexual relationship. It's harder to be one if you're not the only one. God designed sex to bond husband and wife together as one. Don't waste its power on some guy or girl you're not going to stick with forever. Remember, the only guaranteed way to know for sure is marriage.

The Ghost of Relationships Past

Since the act of sex is the act of becoming one flesh with another person, you wind up carrying those past lovers with you into your marriage relationship. If you are thinking about having sex before marriage, think about this: Are you willing to live with the memories? I've heard married couples talk about the difficulties of having great sex with their spouses because of the ghosts of the past relationships that haunt their memories. It's not easy to get rid of them.

I was speaking in a high school in Madison, Wisconsin. As usual, I told them that the best way to have a great sex life was to marry virgins and to remain virgins themselves until marriage. There was a freshman girl there who did not at all like what I was saying. Afterward she came up to talk with me (or rather, talk *at* me).

"I'm not a virgin," she said, as her little underdeveloped body trembled with rage, "and I don't want to marry a virgin." She seemed to be taking pride in her own defiance.

I asked her, "Do you want your future husband comparing your chest size to someone else's? Or how well you perform in bed to someone else?"

"No," she said sheepishly. As we talked her countenance began to change. She walked off pondering the reality that had just hit her between the eyes. She had been challenged, and knew she was wrong.

The Gift That Keeps on Giving

Premarital sex can have a devastating effect. But what's even worse, it can kill you and your future family too. In a moment of passionate indulgence you can walk away with something that will stay with you and haunt you forever, something that sets you up an appointment with the "grim reaper."

Look at just a few of the facts from the Medical Institute for Sexual Health:

▼

People who run school clinics that distribute free condoms know that these things don't work to prevent pregnancy in teenagers. At least 20 percent of the girls who rely on condoms for birth control get pregnant within a year or so.

▼

In the 1960s syphilis and gonorrhea were the only two serious sexually transmitted diseases (STDs). Only a generation later, there are twenty prevalent sexually transmitted diseases, and fifty overall. There are twelve million newly infected persons each year. Syphilis and gonorrhea can be treated with penicillin, but there is no cure for many of these new viral diseases.

Eighty percent of those infected experience no noticeable symptoms, and so have no idea they are carriers of a contagious, sexually transmitted disease.

▼

It is estimated that one in five Americans is now infected with a viral STD, and that doesn't include the bacterial diseases such as syphilis and gonorrhea.

▼

The most tragic thing about these numbers is that 63 percent of these infections occur in persons under the age of twenty-five.

▼

Teenagers have a higher degree of susceptibility than do older people. Researchers have estimated that a sexually active fifteen-year-old has a one-in-eight chance of developing pelvic inflammatory disease. That's ten times greater than it is for a woman who is twenty-four.

▼

Condoms have been found to have a 31 percent failure rate in preventing the sexual transmission of the HIV virus, and that percentage is based only on the cases that have been reported. The actual failure rate is certainly higher.

▼

The human papilloma virus (HPV) is probably the most common sexually transmitted disease in America. Dr. Stephen Curry of the New England Medical Center in Boston was quoted in

Time: "This virus is rampant. If it were not for AIDS, stories about it would be on the front page of every newspaper." HPV has become the number-one reason American women visit a gynecologist, according to the Center for Disease Control. HPV is the precipitating agent for the vast majority of cancers of the cervix, vagina, and penis.

Dr. Alex M. Ferenczy, Professor of Pathology, Obstetrics, and Gynecology at McGill University, stated, "Of all STDs, HPV is the greatest cancer killer. Nearly 500,000 women each year worldwide develop cancer of the cervix."

Several studies have shown that condoms DO NOT protect against the HPV virus.[2]

▼

How safe is "safe sex"? Most researchers feel there may be no such thing as safe sex. The failure rate of condoms is one-in-five in preventing pregnancies, even with the fact that a girl can get pregnant only a few days a month when she ovulates. Think of the failure rate in preventing AIDS and other sexually transmitted diseases when a person is vulnerable every day of the month! Condoms are only tested for holes or defects ten microns or larger. The HIV virus is less than one-tenth of a micron in size. The HIV virus passing through a ten-micron hole is equivalent to throwing a golf ball through a fifteen-foot circle. How safe does that sound to you?

The truth is that the whole "safe sex" campaign being aggressively promoted to teenagers is the biggest myth of all, and the scientific community knows it. P.R. Redfied of Walter Reed Army Hospital said, "Sex with a condom can only be described as dangerous sex."[3]

Premarital sex can have a devastating effect in so many ways. It can even kill you or leave you with a painful reminder for the rest of your life. How would you like for your future mate to be reminded of your premarital sexual adventures every time you have to treat your disease? Is all this really worth one night of pleasure?

5 ▼ No Rules, Just Right

I t has become so politically incorrect these days to talk about sin that fewer and fewer people even understand the concept. So, let's define what it is. *Sin: to miss the mark, to offend, to violate, or to break God's law.* Another word for sin is transgression. A sinner is a transgressor. The word "transgress" comes from two Latin words, one meaning to cross, and the other to step. So to sin is to step over the line.

Lines are drawn and boundaries are set in all relationships. When people transgress, they step over the line and sin against one another, against the civil law, or against the law of God. So when it comes to sexual transgression, the question is: Who draws the line, and where is it?

People try to deal with the sin issue in their lives in all kinds of ways. None of these approaches are new. They're just recycled old ideas people have used for centuries in an effort to avoid facing this most uncomfortable truth. You're probably familiar with all of them, but let's identify a few.

The Devil Made Me Do It!

We are becoming a generation of victims who blame everything on something or someone else. If you believe what the social evolutionists say, then we are merely products of our environment, and whatever we do, good or bad, can be blamed on somebody else—or even everybody else. I saw an article in the paper about the two kids who have been convicted of murdering Michael Jordan's father. The suggestion was that since they had a difficult childhood, they were somehow "less guilty" for their cold-blooded murder. Increasingly, that is the way people think.

Unfortunately, the average kid today thinks more and more like the guests on a daytime talk show. Everyone's griping and whining; few ever take responsibility for their own actions. This ability to blame others for one's own failures is characteristic of our post-Christian culture. Some go so far as to blame evil forces at work, from a cookie-stealing kid who protests, "The devil made me do it," to the serial killer who states that demons told him to murder.

The fact that people have become so adept at making excuses doesn't mean that they actually have valid excuses, especially when it comes to stepping across God's line. There are a few places in the Bible, particularly in the Book of Romans, that tell us about people and their excuses.

Whatever is written in these Scriptures is not what God says about others but to us to whom these Scriptures were addressed in the first place! And it's clear enough, isn't it, that we're sinners, every one of us, in the same sinking boat with everybody else.   ROMANS 3:19, THE MESSAGE

Some people go through the mental exercise of what they are going to say to justify themselves when they stand before God. But on that day there will be nothing to say, because God knows the depths of people's hearts better than they do. Even to those people who would say that they didn't know about the Ten Commandments or about the lines of sexual transgression, the Bible says:

> When outsiders who have never heard of God's law follow it more or less by instinct, they confirm its truth by their obedience. They show that God's law is not something alien, imposed on us from without, but woven into the very fabric of our creation. There is something deep within them that echoes God's yes and no, right and wrong. Their response to God's yes and no will become public knowledge on the day God makes his final decision about every man and woman.
>
> ROMANS 2:14-16, THE MESSAGE

All of our excuses are only justified in our own minds. Sooner or later, everyone will find that out.

The Psychological Side Step

It's OK for psychologists to talk about *feelings* of guilt. But the next time the subject comes up in a sociology or psychology class, try bringing up the concept of *real* guilt and watch the sparks fly. The discussion will heat up in no time.

You see, if what we have to deal with are only our own feelings of guilt, then all we have to do to get rid of them is convince ourselves that sin is just a social convention. It's not real, just a bad trip some past generation has laid on us. If we can convince ourselves there is no such thing as real sin, then, hey, there's no real guilt either. It's only in our imaginations, and we can dismiss it.

In other words, for many people it's easier to say, *"There is no God, so there is no such thing as sin!"* than it is to deal with their own transgressions. As usual, we can find a description of such people in the Bible:

> For since the creation of the world, his invisible attributes, his eternal power, and divine nature have been clearly seen, being understood through what has been made, so that they are without excuse. For even though they knew God, they did not honor him as God, or give thanks; but they became futile in their speculations, and their foolish heart was darkened. Professing to be wise they became fools.   ROMANS 1:20-22

This means that even without the benefit of the Bible, human beings are able to figure out that God is a powerful creator with clear requirements for right living. And yet, even with all that proof, sidesteppers try to erase the plain truth of right and wrong by denying the existence of God. The trouble is that they don't have a valid excuse for missing the point.

Legal Loopholes

It's amazing how creative the average person can be when necessary. Those who are even vaguely familiar with the Bible know that it says that fornication (premarital sex) and adultery are sins against God. People who are regularly having premarital sex justify it by saying, "But we *really* love each other." People who have cheated on their mates make excuses by saying, "But we *really didn't* love each other!" Somehow that's supposed to make it OK.

The goal of psychological sidestepping is to find legal-sounding loopholes (reasonable-sounding excuses) so that you can get away with doing what you want to do.

Cut Loose from Law

Some people take a very theological approach in an attempt to justify their sinning. They point out the fact that the Bible says that Jesus set us free from the Old Testament Law of Moses, and now we are under a new covenant of grace. We are, in fact, free from the old Jewish Law, but their distorted interpretation is that they are now free to do anything they want without any moral restrictions. This is really an old heresy call "antinomianism," which means "without law." To their way of thinking, "justification by faith" becomes "just-a-vacation-by-faith."

Jesus said, "Do not think that I came to abolish the Law or the Prophets; I did not come to abolish, but to fulfill" (Matthew 5:17). The New Testament or New Covenant eliminates much of the ceremonial law the Jews had observed. But it does not do away with moral law. In fact, under the New Covenant we are closer to the law of God than ever before because, if you are a Christian, the Spirit of the Lawgiver lives right inside of you.

Even if a person technically keeps the Ten Commandments, it doesn't mean that he or she is right with God. A rich young ruler came to Jesus. To his way of thinking, he had kept all the commandments. So he asked Jesus what he still lacked in order to enter the kingdom of God. Did he really want to know? Maybe he just wanted to hear Jesus say what a great person he was because he had been so careful to follow the Ten Commandments. On the other hand, perhaps he did sense that something very important was missing in his life. Jesus' response was, "Sell all you have and follow me." Jesus didn't tell everyone to sell everything and follow him. To some he just said, "Go and sin no more." Jesus had a way of touching the very issue in a person's life that represented the idol of his or her heart.

He still does the same thing today. You see, one of the commandments was to worship God and serve him only. The rich young ruler had probably done all the things he needed to do to technically fulfill that requirement. But Jesus saw more deeply into his heart. He saw that money was the rich young man's idol; it was what he served. To all appearances, he had obeyed the Ten Commandments, but in fact he had violated the spirit of the Law.

Idolatry isn't just bowing and worshiping a statue. The Bible says, "Therefore consider the members of your earthly body as dead to immorality, impurity, evil desire and greed, which amounts to idolatry" (Galatians 3:5). Idolatry can be anything that you put before God: money, career, a goal, or even a relationship.

Some people who would never think of worshiping another god have, in effect, set up their girlfriend or boyfriend as their idol. The Holy Spirit may be convicting you on this very point: who or what are the idols in your life? Following or not following Jesus hinges on your willingness to put away your idols. Often we think of all the bad things we put before God. But he does not want us to put *anything* before him, whether it be good or bad.

The Law in Our Hearts

God is not naive. He isn't fooled by people who try to circumvent what is morally right. He peers right into the depths of a person's heart. Listen to the words of Jesus from the Sermon on the Mount:

You have heard that it was said, "You shall not commit adultery"; but I say to you that everyone who looks on a woman to lust for her has committed adultery with her already in his heart.   MATTHEW 5:27-28

You see, in God's eyes, right and wrong are not just what you do, what people can see, but the secret stuff—what you allow in your heart and mind.

The word conscience comes from two words, "con" meaning "with" and "science" meaning "to know." God has given us a conscience "to know with." Webster defines the conscience as "an awareness of right and wrong, with a compulsion to do right." Our conscience is a sensitive alarm that reminds us of God's holy standards. When we start to do something wrong, that alarm goes off. The conscience's inner voice says, "Stop this! This is wrong! Don't do this!"

A college girl wrote to a popular Christian magazine:

I was raised in a good Christian home. I was always taught that sex before marriage was wrong. When my boyfriend and I began to get involved sexually, I felt guilty at first. Before long, I couldn't understand why I ever felt bad at all.

She went on to say that she and her boyfriend were living together at college. What was wrong with this confused college girl? Why had her standards changed so drastically? Had her parents deceived her by saying that sex outside of marriage was wrong?

This girl's problem and confusion came from two sources. The Bible says that there is pleasure in sin for a season (Hebrews

11:25). She must have believed the logic, "It feels too right to be wrong."

When you start to sin, it may seem exciting, daring, and pleasurable, but there is always a high price to pay later. A friend of mine put it this way, "Sin will take you farther than you want to go, keep you longer than you want to stay, and cost you more than you want to pay!" Someone else said, "Sin comes as a guest, promises to stay as a friend, declares you to be the master, but, in the end, only makes you its slave."

The problem with how this girl felt about her sin is that she had ignored the warnings of her conscience for so long that she could no longer hear its sensitive alarm. If we listen to our consciences, we become more sensitive to God's voice as he lovingly seeks to guide and direct our lives. If we ignore our consciences, it gets harder and harder to hear and do what is right.

It's as if those who regularly ignore God's Spirit speaking to their hearts "sear" or "brand" their consciences (1 Timothy 4:2). It's like branding a cow. Ranchers say that you can take a long needle, stick it in the spot where the cow has been branded, and the cow can't even feel it. This is exactly what happens to your heart when you ignore your conscience. That college girl's heart was so callous that she no longer felt the guilt. She lost the ability to know the difference between right and wrong. Instead of feeling afraid for her mistake she simply felt "free." This free feeling leads to a false sense of peace. Don't let it happen to you.

Here are some questions to ask yourself to see where you stand with your conscience:

- Are you doing things now that you said you would never do?

- Was there ever a time when you criticized others for doing what you are now doing?

- Have you allowed a guy or girl to wear down the alarm of your conscience by going further and further sexually each time you are alone together?

- Have you justified the guilt you feel by comparing yourself to others? *I'm not as bad as they are. You wouldn't believe what they do!*

If the answer to any of these questions is "yes," then you are on the road to losing both the sensitivity of your conscience and the power it gives you to do what is right.

Matters of the Heart

God's source book, the Bible, has a lot to say about sex—not only the physical act, but the mental aspects of sexual transgression. In the Book of Galatians we find these words:

For the flesh lusts against the Spirit, and the Spirit against the flesh; and these are contrary to one another, so that you cannot do the things that you would. But if you are led by the Spirit, you are not under the law. Now the works of the flesh are manifest, which are these: adultery, fornication, uncleanliness, lasciviousness, idolatry… as I have told you in times past, that they which do such things will not inherit the Kingdom of God.   GALATIANS 5:17-21, THE MESSAGE

Adultery, when it is mentioned in the Bible, usually refers to a married person who is involved sexually with someone other than his or her spouse. Sometimes the words "adultery" and "fornication" are used interchangeably. But most often when both words are used as you see here, adultery refers to married sexual immorality and fornication refers to premarital sex.

"Why is sex such a big deal in the Bible?" some ask. The reason the Bible says so much about it is that when you step over the line sexually, you sin in multiple directions. You sin or transgress against yourself, against the person with whom you are involved sexually, against your future marriage partner, against your parents, against your children, and most importantly, against God and his purpose for creating sex.

I was reading Galatians 5:17 at the beginning of one of my messages on "Dating, Love, and Sex," and I got to the part that says, "They which do such things will not inherit the kingdom of God." I was talking about sexual sin and how it can affect our eternal destiny. As if that had never occurred to her before, a girl in the back row shrieked, "Is that really true?" You see, we hear so much about "safe sex" and so little about God's Word that many teenagers don't know that sex outside of marriage is wrong. And God didn't say it was wrong just to spoil your fun. Besides the fact that the prohibited sexual activity transgresses many lines, God said it was wrong because he knew that fornication and adultery would keep you from having a sex life that he intended, one that is "very good"! And God wants you to be with him in heaven—he really does.

Four Ways to Get Lascivious

That same verse in Galatians exposes other sexual sins which can rob us of heaven's happiness, sins such as uncleanliness and lasciviousness. Lasciviousness is also translated as "sexuality" in the Bible. It means, in simple terms, turning yourself on sexually or intentionally turning someone else on. That happens in several different ways.

Turned On by Pornography

You don't find pornography only in *Playboy* anymore. You can find it in rock magazines, you can find it on network or cable television, and you can find it in almost any PG-13 movie.

Pornography is addictive, and people who have been hooked find that it destroys their ability to enjoy normal sex in their marriage. Like those who are addicted to powerful narcotics, porno addicts need to find material that is increasingly kinky in order to get turned on. After having made their way through the hardcore porno scene, people in this kind of bondage very often wind up involved in some kind of perverted, sado-masochistic sex in order to stimulate themselves. They've burned themselves out on pornography. In almost every case the extreme perversion of serial killers and sexual predators began with pornography.

Guys, you can be the strongest Christian in the world, but you can't see some bare-chested girl run around on the screen and not have it affect you. God created you in such a way that it will affect you. That's why it's important for you to protect yourself. David wrote, "I will walk within my house in the integrity of my heart. I will set no worthless thing before my eyes" (Psalms 101:2-3, NAB). Job said, "I have made a covenant with my eyes.

Why should I gaze intently upon a young woman?"

Jesus taught in the Sermon on the Mount that lusting after a woman with your eyes was in effect committing adultery with her in your heart. (The same thing would apply to girls lusting after guys.) He went on like this:

> And if your right eye makes you stumble, tear it out, and throw it from you; for it is better for you that one of the parts of your body perish, than for your whole body to be thrown into hell.
> MATTHEW 5:29, NAB

Pretty radical, wouldn't you say? I don't recommend that you start plucking your eyes out, but you've got to get radical with things in your life that are causing you to stumble, whether it's movies, magazines, places you go, or the people you are with. If you know what you see is turning you on and causing you to stumble, *get rid of it.*

Hand-to-Hand Combat

We used to call it "making out," "getting lip," or "sucking face." You know what I mean: checking out the tonsils. People always ask me, "Well, how far is too far?" Kissing is too far for some people. Anything that sexually arouses you is too far for you. *Whenever you stir up a desire you cannot fulfill with the blessings of God, that's too far.*

Sex is like a bomb with a long fuse on it. When kids get sexually aroused, they burn a little bit of that fuse. But the next time the burned part of that fuse isn't replaced. You pick up right where you left off, and it burns a little farther. Then the next time, and the next time, and before you know it, there are only a few scant centimeters left on your fuse.

What happens is that you have stirred up a desire that should not be stirred up until God says, "OK, this is the person." At the right time you can light the fuse and let the fireworks begin. That time is when the marriage covenant is sealed. Otherwise, it is called lasciviousness or stirring yourself up sexually. Lasciviousness is a robber that will keep you from God's best for your sex life. It will also bring addictions you will struggle with for a lifetime.

Turned on by Masturbation

In a survey of 100,000 women, well over 80 percent said that they were involved in masturbation, most of them frequently. In these findings, 54 percent of the women began by the age of fifteen, and 32 percent before that, between the ages of ten and fifteen. In another survey, 80 percent of males under the age of twenty-four claimed to be involved in masturbation. I'm going to give you three scriptural reasons on why masturbation is a sin.

Number one: Masturbation is a sin because it involves fantasy. When people are masturbating they are not meditating on watermelons. The Bible says, "As a man thinks in his heart so is he." If you are involved in arousing yourself sexually and you are thinking of some girl's chest or some guy's body, then that is sin.

Number two: Masturbation is a lack of self-control. Self-control is a fruit of the Spirit. You can't have the Spirit of God and another spirit moving through you at the same time. Both spirits can be drawing you, but your actions are a response to one or the other.

When you masturbate, you're casting off self-control and allowing lust to control you.

Number three: Masturbation is an unnatural way of satisfying a God-given desire. Premarital sex is also an unnatural way of satisfying a God-given desire. So is gluttony. Almost all lust is simply a perversion of a God-given desire. Sin is a wrong way of fulfilling that desire.

Turned on by Defrauding

To defraud means to make a promise or arouse an expectation that you cannot or will not fulfill. People regularly defraud one another in business. Lasciviousness is to defraud someone sexually by arousing desires you cannot righteously fulfill.

Girls, don't be naive. You need to understand that guys are turned on more easily than you are by what they *see*. Girls can defraud a guy by the way they dress. Whether you're wearing a swimsuit, shorts, jeans, or a formal, there is a difference between looking good and attempting to turn someone on sexually.

You can also defraud people sexually by the way you act. I've been around youth groups for a long time, and there's no counting how many times I've seen girls come, jump up on some guy's lap, and say, "Hi, how are you doing?"

The truth is that a lot of people flirt because stirring up other people sexually is like a game to them. They may not even like the person, but it is very satisfying to think that another person is turned on sexually by them. It's like a little trophy.

People also defraud each other emotionally, even if they do not cross the line physically. Looking for a new emotional thrill, they say, "I love you," "Let's go steady," or, "Let's get engaged."

That may give 'em a buzz for awhile. However, we're not only to save our bodies for the one we marry, we're to save our heart as well.

Most of the new Christians in the church in Thessalonica had previously been a part of pagan religions that had no restrictions whatsoever against sexual immorality. (Sounds like man-made religion, doesn't it?) This is what the Apostle Paul wrote to them:

> For you know what commandments we gave you by the authority of the Lord Jesus. For this is the will of God, your sanctification; that is, that you abstain from sexual immorality; that each of you know how to possess his own vessel in sanctification and honor, not in lustful passion, like the Gentiles who do not know God; and that no man transgress and defraud his brother in the matter.   1 THESSALONIANS 4:2-6 (italics mine)

The Bible is pretty clear about the lines of sexual purity. God gives rules, not just because he's a big boss, but because they are right. He's given us the wonderful and powerful gift of sex. He also gave us some guidelines so we wouldn't mess it all up and destroy ourselves with it.

6 ▼ You're Entitled to Love

A lot of people are remembered for either the one big thing they did right or the one big thing they did wrong. You've heard the Nike commercial about some great athletes who, though mere humans, on certain days played as if they were perfect. For instance, in the sixth and deciding game of the 1977 World Series, Reggie Jackson hit three consecutive homers, each one off the first pitch. In a single NBA game, Michael Jordan once poured in sixty-three points. Joe Montana once passed to Dwight Clark for a touchdown in the Super Bowl, a play that has come to be simply known as "The Catch."

It would be great to be remembered by the best day you've ever had. But how would you like to be forever memorialized by the greatest mistake or the most embarrassing moment of your life? There are some players who, no matter how many other great things they accomplished, will always be remembered by their biggest blooper.

"Shoeless" Joe Jackson was one of the greatest players to step onto a baseball field. After over seventy-five years, he still holds the third-highest lifetime batting average. But he will always be remembered as one of the eight Chicago White Sox players who took a bribe to throw the 1919 World Series. Jackson was banned from baseball for life.

Bill Buckner played twenty-two years in the major leagues, and had an impressive lifetime batting average of .289. But what most people remember about Buckner is the sixth game of the 1986 World Series between Buckner's Boston Red Sox and the New York Mets. The score was tied at the bottom of the tenth inning, with two outs and a runner on third. Mookie Wilson hit an easy, routine ground ball down the first base line. All Buckner had to do was field the ball, touch first base, and the Red Sox would win the World Series. Unbelievably, the ball went right between Buckner's legs, enabling Ray Knight to score from third base. The Mets won the sixth game to tie the series and game seven to become world champions. In addition to Buckner's error the Red Sox organization will also continue to be known for their biggest mistake—they traded Babe Ruth to the Yankees and haven't won the World Series since.

There's a person in the Bible who is most remembered for his big mistake. His name is Esau. The story goes like this: the son of Abraham, Isaac, and his wife, Rebekah, had twins, Esau and Jacob. Esau was very athletic and a great outdoorsman. He wasn't too smart, though; Esau was the dumb jock of the twentieth century B.C. His brother was a cunning, nerdy little kid who was sort of a couch potato. He hung around the tents with his mom all the time.

Now, Isaac really loved his athletic son better than Jacob. He probably went to all of Esau's Little League games and screamed like a wild man every time he came up to bat. This didn't go unnoticed by Jacob, who began thinking of ways to get even with his brother.

An opportunity presented itself one afternoon when Esau came in from a hunting trip, famished. Jacob had his pot of soup cooking. "Brother, please, let me have a swallow of some of that red stuff," asked Esau.

"First sell me your birthright," Jacob said, ready to seize the opportunity. The birthright represented Esau's inheritance. As the oldest son, he would receive the majority of his father's wealth.

"Behold, I am about to die," said Esau. "What use then is the birthright to me?"

"First swear to me," Jacob persisted.

So he swore to him, and sold his birthright to Jacob. Then Jacob gave Esau bread and lentil stew; and he ate and drank, and rose and went on his way. Thus Esau despised his birthright.   GENESIS 25:33-34

(If you've ever eaten lentil soup, you'll agree that this was a bad deal any way you look at it.)

For people who live in a twentieth-century democracy, it's hard to appreciate the significance of the birthright. The laws that have for thousands of years governed the right of succession of monarchies have their origins in the ancient family birthright system, under which the oldest son was destined to received a double portion of his father's inheritance and would be the patriarch or leader of the clan. He would possess great authority and honor. Esau traded away his right to all that in a famished moment.

Think of the British monarchy. Charles, the Prince of Wales, is in the line of succession to the throne after his mother, Queen Elizabeth. What Esau did would be comparable to Prince Charles coming in from a polo match so hungry that he traded his right to be king to his little brother, Andrew, for a big juicy hamburger. It would be stupid.

To say that Esau "despised his birthright" doesn't necessarily mean he didn't want to have it. It simply means that he didn't understand or appreciate the value of it. He was so shortsighted that he valued something to satisfy his immediate appetite more than his most valuable possession. Listen to what the New Testament says about it.

See to it that no one misses the grace of God and that no bitter root grows up to cause trouble and defile many. See that no one is sexually immoral, or is godless like Esau, who for a single meal sold his inheritance rights as the oldest son. Afterward, as you know, when he wanted to inherit this blessing, he was rejected. He could bring about no change of mind, though he sought the blessing with tears.

HEBREWS 12:15-17, NIV

Your Greatest Gift

I guess you can see where I'm going with this. People exchange the greatest wedding gift they have to give their future husband or wife for a moment of passion, for a temporary relationship, or for fear of what others think. Listen, girls and guys, you have a special gift to give to the person you are going to marry. Like Esau, who sought with tears to regain his birthright, if you give away your virginity ahead of time, you can't get it back. If you're beautiful, beauty can't buy it back. If you're rich, money can't buy it back. If you're Miss America... none of those things will buy back that one gift for which every person waits.

How are you going to feel if you find out that you are the fourth, the fifth, the tenth, or that they've lost count. Really special, huh?

Patrick is a youth minister and a friend of mine who waited for marriage to have sex. When Pat met Lisa he was twenty-five years old. They grew to be deeply in love. The day arrived when Pat was ready to ask Lisa to marry him. Lisa looked at him with a concerned expression. They had talked a little about their past lives. But Pat had no idea how much Lisa had been sexually involved before she became a Christian. As Lisa began to share the story of living with different guys through years of premarital sexual activity, Pat's heart was completely broken. For weeks, he cried and prayed. He just felt so cheated.

Pat still loved Lisa and wanted to marry her, but he was confused and hurt, having a very difficult time accepting Lisa's past. Pat had waited his whole life. He had preached about it, and encouraged many others to stay sexually pure. But now the one he had chosen, the one with whom he wanted to share this special gift, had not waited for him. The wedding plans were put on hold while Pat prayed and sought counseling.

Finally, Pat broke through his pain by remembering the Scripture, "If anyone is in Christ, he is a new creation; old things have passed away; behold all things are made new" (2 Corinthians 5:17, NKJV). Meditating on this Scripture and others like it helped Pat and Lisa to heal this difficult hurt. After talking things through and praying together, they finalized their date and were married. No one knows better than these two the regrets of being sexually involved before marriage.

It's like God has given you a treasure chest. Each time you are involved sexually you give a part of that treasure away. You rob the one who may have been saving a whole treasure just for you.

What if you both dip into your treasure chests before marriage, even with each other? Isn't that sort of like keeping the treasure "in the family," a bit more than it is to be doing something wrong? Good point. However, it's well documented that couples who have been involved with each other before marriage trust each other less than couples who wait for marriage. You need to know that giving sexual "favors" to anyone, including your intended husband or wife, affects you negatively. As one girl put it:

> Think of yourself in a room with a circle of people and two beautiful roses. One of the roses is passed around, with each person taking a petal from the blossom. The other rose is saved and kept especially for your one true love. When the first rose has come full circle, it has been touched so much that its beauty has been lost forever. The second rose is untouched, and its beauty remains for the one to whom it was meant to be given.

> This is the story my mother told me when I asked if it was all right to have sex with my boyfriend. She asked me if I wanted to be like the first rose or remain fresh and beautiful for the one I was meant to be given to, the man I would one day marry. I made the decision to wait, and my experience with my husband on our wedding night wasn't just sex. It was a first-time beautiful love. A love we both had saved just for each other.

The Power of Pride and Purpose

Would you want someone to give you his or her most costly possession? Your response, of course, would all depend on the net worth of the giver. If the giver was a zillionaire, it could be quite significant, but if a pauper, you probably wouldn't waste your time with it. We all have one particularly valuable gift to give— our virginity. When people easily give in to sexual temptation or intimidation, it is often because they don't understand how valuable they are as human beings or how precious that one gift they have to give is.

One of the greatest blessings of your entire life will be giving yourself mind, soul, and body to the person with whom you'll spend the rest of your life. As I said before, true love gives (and can wait). Lust only takes (and the sooner the better!).

A lot of kids are like Esau—they get involved sexually, trading in the gift of their virginity for something they want or even feel like they desperately need. Afterward when they step back and look at what they've done, they realize how much, in the passion of the moment, they traded for so little.

Teenagers are not generally known for long-range thinking, but their problem is not necessarily intelligence. Often the greater issue that weakens teenagers' resolve has more to do with self-esteem and self-worth. They greatly overestimate the value of sex and what it will do for them, and they greatly underestimate their own self-worth and the value of that one special gift they have to give. Consequently, they make a very bad trade.

What enables some kids to remain virgins until the day they are married? Two of the strongest motivating factors are (1) a sense of personal purpose and (2) an accurate sense of personal self-esteem. Most people have hopes and dreams for their own happiness. But just because a guy is determined to be the CEO of a Fortune 500 company or a point guard in the NBA doesn't mean he has enough of a life-purpose, because those life goals center around himself.

Olympians give years of their lives to training. They get up early and stay up late. They study the greatest athletes in their event. They give up years to self-discipline while others around them go right on with comparatively little discipline or sacrifice.

Why do they do this? Do they have something you and I physically do not have? Of course not. The difference is, they have a goal, a dream, a purpose that causes them to discipline themselves from doing many things others are doing who do not have the same goals.

The greatest and highest purpose for your life is far greater than yourself—something worth giving your life for. It is building a healthy sense of self-esteem, discovering what it is God wants us to do with our lives.

Some people have a false sense of self-esteem. They think they are God's gift to the world, and that everyone should bow down at their feet. That's not the kind of purpose and self-esteem I'm talking about. People with this sort of self-perception are very often as self-indulgent and shortsighted as Esau. Without the help of God and the Bible, people's self-estimation usually jumps off the tracks into one extreme (having no self-worth, no sense of purpose) or the other (being consumed with self).

The Foundation of Self-Esteem and Purpose

You may have heard the joke about a mother who told her daughter, "You know, you were an accident."

The girl replied, "No, *you're* the accident. I was supposed to be born rich and beautiful to the family across the street."

Some people are lucky enough to be born good-looking, smart, rich, and talented. I guess I wasn't very lucky because I didn't get any of those gifts. Like a lot of people, on the outside I acted bold and confident, but on the inside I was eaten up with fear and insecurity. Of course, I've talked to thousands of teenagers who live in mansions and drive their own $35,000 cars. These kids are just as messed up as average teens. Sometimes, they are even *more* messed up.

Self-worth is not about money. I know kids who are almost as poor as I was growing up but who have an unshakable estimation of their own value as a person. It's not about success. Some people work hard to feel better about themselves. Others work hard *because* they have healthy self-esteem. Guess which one feels satisfied at the end of the day?

A lot of the things people hang on to for their identity and self-esteem are very tentative, and they can slip away very quickly. But there is one unchanging bedrock truth on which you can stand: (1) God created you, (2) he loves you regardless of what you have done, (3) he has bought you for his own possession by his death on the cross, and (4) he has a unique purpose for your life. *That*, my friends, makes each one of you immensely valuable.

Educators try valiantly to help teenagers feel better about themselves. Most of you have gone through some kind of instruction on self-actualization, defined as the process of realizing the value of yourself. Of course, it's kind of comical listening to people try to come up with some independent value for each individual without using the G-word—GOD. It's even more difficult for them to talk about sin and forgiveness. They usually wind up saying, "I'm OK and you're OK," but that really doesn't take away our guilt or our sins.

A solid sense of self-worth comes from the understanding that God created us, and, even though we were guilty and have a sinful nature, God redeemed us for himself by the death and resurrection of his Son, Jesus Christ. It was quite an uneven exchange, the sinless Son of God for you and me!

You're Entitled to Love

My life changed radically when I met Jesus Christ. The man who introduced me to Christ used to always tell me how special I was, how strongly he felt that God had a unique plan for my life, and how great I was going to be. I kept looking around trying to figure out who he was talking about. It couldn't have been *me*... I had such a low sense of self-worth, it took awhile before I could believe this man was sincere in what he was saying.

If anyone was ever born as an accident, it would have had to have been me. But there are no accidents with God. I don't care if you were conceived in the back seat of a '67 Chevy parked on an old dirt road, then abandoned and raised in foster homes—God has a plan and purpose for you. And part of that plan and purpose might just be a person who is going to be crazy about you, someone who will love you enough to commit the rest of his or her life to you. That's the person for whom you need to save yourself. And when you give yourself to that person, it is with the blessing of God, your parents, and everyone who loves and has invested in both of you. (For those who have a special calling or desire to stay single, your sexual purity is just as important as for someone who will one day marry.)

I've heard the question many times: *If both of us agree to have sex, and we're not hurting anyone else, then what's wrong with it?* Well, the truth is you *are* hurting someone else because you're giving away what should only belong to that person in the future, after your marriage. But there's an even greater reason why it's wrong. Whether you ever get married or not, whether you believe it or not, whether you act like it or not, each one of us is not only created by God, but we have been redeemed (bought back) by him as well. Without Jesus' death on the cross, I would still be lost. But now I'm God's property, and I can't go around giving myself away outside of his purpose. Sex outside marriage is not just a sin against another person; it is a sin against God. Listen to what the Bible says:

> Flee immorality. Every other sin that a man commits is outside the body, but the immoral man sins against his own body. Or do you not know that your body is a temple of the Holy Spirit who is in you, whom you have from God, and that you are not your own? For you have been bought with a price: therefore glorify God in your body.   1 CORINTHIANS 6:18-20

Don't Get Ripped Off

The first time I ever spoke at her church, Laura really stood out in the crowd. She was one of those beautiful girls who looked as if she had just stepped out of a fashion magazine. Her bright blue eyes and warm smile were like magnets that always drew people's attention.

Laura and Rob had been going steady for about three years and they were soon to be married. Just before the wedding date everyone noticed that she was gaining a lot of weight. This was not at all like the petite Laura who always looked so perfect. The wedding day came and went. Seven months later Laura had a baby girl. Nearly a year later someone told me that she had cut off her long beautiful hair, gained about fifty pounds, and was not taking very good care of herself. Soon after that Laura was seeking treatment for an alcohol problem.

What happened? About two months before the wedding, Laura had lost her self-respect (and, presumably, her virginity). With self-worth devastated by sexual sin, she thought, *What difference does it make anymore?* Some people go to that extreme, neglecting or even abusing themselves, while others try to compensate for their inner pain with clothes and makeup.

A "DO NOT ENTER" sign on the Interstate exit ramp is not there to destroy your fun. It's to keep you from destroying yourself and a lot of other innocent people. God wants us to have abundant life, and the rules are to keep us from going the wrong way. Jesus said, "The thief (Satan) comes only to steal, and kill, and destroy; I came that they might have life, and might have it more abundantly" (John 10:10, NAB). Some people have the mental picture of God as an old codger sitting in heaven who can't wait to whack anyone daring to have any fun. That's not true.

Satan's agenda from the very beginning has been to destroy our relationship with God. He also wants to mess with our most important human relationship, our marriage relationship. Through sin he wants to sidetrack us from our purpose. Whenever we yield to temptation, we walk away from our relationship with God, and our true sense of self-worth lessens.

There's good news, though. That's what the word "gospel" means—good news. Regardless of what you have done or what has been done to you to mess it up, God still wants you to have life and have it more abundantly. God is in the business of restoring broken relationships, putting people back on track with regard to the purpose and plan for their lives, and most of all, cleansing people from their past mistakes, failure, and sins. He also wants to help you restore and rebuild the gift you have to give for the special person you will commit your life to in marriage. The Bible says, "'Come now, and let us reason together,' says the Lord, 'though your sins are as scarlet, they will be as white as snow; though they are red like crimson, they will be like wool'" (Isaiah 1:18). Keep reading, and you'll find out how this can happen for you.

7 ▼ The Truest of True Loves

"Hey, baby, you want to go out to the pond down the road and watch the submarine races?" asks Slick Sam.

"Gee, do they have submarine races down there? That would be nice," says Amy Airhead.

A few minutes later they pull up to the pond, and Amy says, "I don't see anything."

The guy says, "Well, baby, I guess we came on the wrong night." He leans over and gives Amy Airhead a little three-second peck that turns into a three-minute smooch that turns into a thirty minute lip-lock. Now they aren't just sittin' *beside* each other anymore, if you know what I mean. The windows are fogged up, steam's coming out of the tail pipe, and he's checking out her dental work.

With their pulse rate up to about two hundred, he looks at her and between gasps for air says, "Baby, I love you."

Oh, he loves me! Amy says to herself. *We'll have the most beautiful wedding, a quaint little house, and three perfect children. We'll drink coffee every morning, and he'll sing to me every evening as we sit on the front porch watching the sunset.*

Yeah, right, Amy. You must have come from a long line of Airheads.

Love with a Hook in It

When a team plays badly but still comes out on top, the coach will sometimes say, "We won ugly, but a win's a win." That's right, you either win the game or you don't. But you cannot in the same way say, "Love is love." It's not so one-dimensional. In the English language the word "love" can refer to anything from your favorite chewing gum to the most highly valued thing in your life. Let me point out three kinds of I-love-you's.

If-love. The first one I call *if-love.* An if-lover says, "If you do what I want you to do, and if you do it with me, and if you don't tell anybody else, then I love you."

"How long will you if-love me?" asks the potential if-love of his life.

"Forever and ever I'll always if-love you," he says, "as long as you do what I want. But if I no longer want you to be the one doing it, then I'll if-love you no longer."

Because-love. The second kind of love is *because-love.* The because-lover says, "I love you because you are so wonderful." That sounds pretty good, doesn't it? It's a lot better than the if-lover. It takes a lot of because-love to make a relationship work for a lifetime. The most important thing, however, is not how much because-love a guy or a girl has, but what their because-love is because of.

He says, "I love you because you're... so beautiful... so popular... (or even) because you're so easy." A girl might say, "Because... you're so good-looking... you've got a great car... (or even) because you are going to be so rich." The homecoming king and queen may not turn out to be the social climbers everyone thought they would. Ask your parents about people they knew in high school who seemed destined for riches and success but never did much of anything. Fortunes may fade, and beauty no doubt will.

The most important question about because-love is "because of what?" Are the reasons someone says, "I because-love you," the things that will cause that love to last a very long time? Until you're old and wrinkled, missing most of your teeth, driving down the road together (at twenty miles an hour) into the sunset? And you'll think your sweetheart is every bit as gorgeous as the day you were married. That's "because-love."

That's how I feel about my wife. We're both going to get old and wrinkled together. I believe she'll be as beautiful to me then as she is now. But my because-love is because of who she is, not just how she looks.

Real love. The third kind of love is *real love.* Real love says, "I love you (period)." The love I have for my wife isn't merely because-love, but unselfish real love. That's the kind of love that God has for us, one that give unselfishly and unconditionally. It is the highest and the truest of true loves. It's not easy to find someone with such true love, but the best place to look is among those who are filled with the love of God.

The God-Kind of Love

The New Testament was originally written in Greek, and in Greek there are several words used to describe love. *Phileo* is translated "love" in English; it refers to the love between brothers. The word "Philadelphia" means "the city of *phileo*," or "the city of brotherly love."

The second Greek word, which is translated into English as "love", is *eros*. From it we get the word "erotic." You know what that means—sexual passion.

The third Greek word for love is *agape*. *Agape* love is completely unselfish, unconditional, and unending. It is referred to as the love of God. *Agape* love, God's love, seems almost too good to be true.

What is God really like anyway? Well, there's more to know about the nature and character of God than the human mind could contain, but we can start to understand. The Bible tells us a lot about God. He has infinite wisdom, power, and knowledge. He is eternal (always has been and always will be), he is omnipresent (he is everywhere, all the time), and he is full of glory. But with all that the Scriptures say *about* God's attributes, there are only two things that the Bible says that God *is*. First of all, "God is love" (*agape* love—1 John 4:8). The very essence of the unchangeable nature of God is this: he loves unselfishly, unconditionally, and unendingly.

Now before you start thinking that means God is like a grandmother who dotes over you regardless of your attitude or actions, look at the other thing that God is. "God is holy" (1 Peter 1:16). He always, no matter what, chooses and does what is eternally right, holy, and just. Now, that's the scary part, because God is our eternal judge, and if any of us get what we deserve with regard to eternal reward in heaven or hell, we are in the biggest trouble one can be in.

Listen to what the Bible says about the demonstration of God's *agape*-love.

God demonstrates His own love toward us, in that while we were yet sinners, Christ died for us.   ROMANS 5:8, NAB

God sacrificed Jesus on the altar of the world to clear that world of sin. Having faith in him sets us in the clear. God decided on this course of action in full view of the public—to set the world in the clear with himself through the sacrifice of Jesus, finally taking care of the sins he had so patiently endured.   ROMANS 3:25-26, THE MESSAGE

God loves you and wants to forgive your sin, but—and this is his divine dilemma—a God who is both holy and just cannot simply overlook sin. So he decided to demonstrate his *agape*-love for us by sending his Son, Jesus Christ, to die on the cross as a sacrifice for our sins. He forgives us because our sins are totally and completely atoned for (paid for) by the blood of Christ. He was both totally loving and totally just in sending his Son to die for your sin.

God loves unconditionally and unendingly, and he will always unselfishly do what is right. Wouldn't you like to have a husband or a wife who loves you like that? If so (and of course you would), then you will need to marry a godly person, a person who is like God.

A godly man or woman is one whose relationship with you is driven by *agape*-love. This is different than if-love, the ungodly characteristics of which are lust, impatience, selfishness, jealousy, and control. A godly person is also one who has made a lifelong commitment to do what's right in private life, with his friends, his work, his family, and especially with you.

"Easier said than done," you say? Sure, but not impossible. Since it is not in our human nature to act this way, I recommend you look for someone who doesn't rely on his or her human strength alone, but who has God's Spirit living inside. I don't just mean someone who goes to church or says, "I'm a Christian," but someone who is also letting the Holy Spirit control his or her attitudes and actions from within.

There's a hitch: a guy or a girl who is capable of giving *agape*-love is not going to marry someone who is periodically unfaithful and only willing to give if-love. If all I had offered Michelle was a slick-talking, good-looking guy with a nice car and a lot of money, she wouldn't have given me a second thought.

Here's the key, friends: if you want to marry someone who can love you tender and love you true with *agape*-love, you've got to become that person first. Stop looking for the right person to fall in love with. Instead, start becoming the right person someone else can fall in love with. It may be hard to see yourself that way, but you absolutely can be such a person. I'm going to tell you how in the last two chapters.

8 ▾ Contracting a Relationship

Chuck and Terry were a very attractive couple who were already living together when I first met them. Eventually they decided to get married. After the wedding they appeared to be very happy and both very much in love. Everything seemed to be going great—that is, until Chuck began to work long hours. Terry began to feel jealous and neglected. Before long she had found a boyfriend.

What happened in Chuck and Terry's relationship is very common. They released a monster into their relationship before they were ever married. They were unfaithful to God before marriage, and in doing so, they opened the door to unfaithfulness in their marriage.

Someone once said that in the beginning of every relationship are the seeds of its own destruction or of its own success. If you don't get the foundation right from the beginning, it's likely to come apart under pressure. Jesus told a parable about two houses, one built on rock and one built on sand. When winds, rain, and floods came, the house on the rock withstood them. He said about the house on the sand, "It fell, and great was its fall" (Matthew 7:27, THE MESSAGE).

How can you build your house on rock? One of the most important things you can do in a dating relationship is to draw clear guidelines on the very first date. You need to be specific about where you are coming from and how far you are willing to go emotionally, spiritually, and physically.

I can hear a lot of you thinking right now, *You're kidding, Jacob. That would be SO EMBARRASSING!*

Well, why so? Every time two people enter a business relationship they write up a contract. In your classes, there is a syllabus given out on the first day explaining what is expected of you and exactly how you will be graded. In some college classes, teachers actually contract with students for particular grades. Even when I do business with a trusted Christian brother, we draw up a contract. It's not because I don't trust him, but because I value our relationship, and I want to prevent any confusion or misunderstanding. The more I value the relationship, the clearer I want the agreement to be. You see, relationships are destroyed when the parties assume that they understand each other's expectations. If they don't work things out ahead of time, eventually someone crosses the line and violates the assumed agreement and damages the relationship.

When you don't agree on the guidelines of a dating relationship up front, it sends a message that you might be one of those people whose convictions are dependent upon the mood of the moment. Maybe your date will get the idea that though you have convictions, you are keeping your options open. There are a lot of things that can be said by your silence. Besides, it's impossible to start laying a proper foundation after the fact.

I assume that if you have read this far, you are a person who already has some set standards, or at least you're working on some. But people who are too embarrassed to talk about their convictions up front find it even more difficult in the heat of passion to start talking about spiritual things. It's like starting to pour a concrete foundation to your relationship in the middle of a raging storm with three feet of flood water.

Lonely in Love

I met my old girlfriend at church. We were going to church with our families. Both of us were very lonely and didn't feel like anyone cared about us. We were starved for love and affection. Since we were two of a kind, we hit it off right away and started dating. We just hung out alone because we didn't have a lot of friends. It was two years before we had sex. When we finally did, it just kinda happened, I guess because we were alone together all the time.

We each knew it was wrong, but we didn't want to hurt each other's feelings. So it just went on. One thing that bothered me about it was that I didn't trust her. We talked on and off about getting married when she turned eighteen. But I thought if she wouldn't save herself until marriage for me, what would keep her from cheating on me once we were married?

I came to the point where I started getting serious about my relationship with Jesus Christ. It was then that I realized I would never be happy without Jesus and that I needed to get straight. When I told Tracy that our relationship had to change, she started dating other guys. Within a year she ended up marrying some guy because she got pregnant. Then she had a miscarriage and was trying to get a divorce because she really didn't love him.

Bill and Tracy were lonely lovers who wandered into a relationship without a solid foundation. They were either too embarrassed or too uncommitted to talk about any guidelines at the beginning, and then, when they both knew they had crossed over the line, they couldn't confront the issue. Bill eventually realized that their relationship needed to be founded on Jesus Christ. But how much pain they could have avoided if they had started out that way!

Seldom do two people have the exact same expectations on a date. You can leave the other one guessing, and that person will just have to "feel you out." The problem is that when he or she gets to feeling too much, then you have to say something in a way that is usually even more awkward.

Have you ever gotten into a dating relationship and wished that you could go back to that first date and clearly state the guidelines? Let me tell you something; once you stumble over those boundaries it takes a whole lot more courage, conviction, boldness, and willpower to establish them in a relationship. It's like trying to put the toothpaste back into the tube. Can you look back on one of your dating relationships and see that? As things got more and more physical, did you come to a point where you were too embarrassed to lay down your guidelines? Or maybe by that time you felt so guilty yourself that it seemed hypocritical to start preaching values.

On the other hand, how many of you have ever dated someone that laid out the guidelines on the first date? What would that sound like?

"Hey, I don't kiss on the first date. I will never allow you to touch me in a sexual way. I don't believe in premarital sex."

Some of you are thinking, *But saying something like that might really turn 'em off*. Well, maybe some will be turned off, but what's your intention—to really turn 'em on?

I've heard people say, "Well, they know I'm a Christian." I hope you know that doesn't mean the same thing to everybody. Some guys and girls think all that means is that you can ask forgiveness after you have done everything that you wanted to do. You know what most of the girls I used to date told me? "Jacob, you are the first guy that I have ever dated who was a Christian that ever acted like it."

If you really value a potential relationship, you'll start it with some guidelines and build it on solid rock. Remember, in the beginning of every relationship are the seeds of its own destruction or of its own success.

"I'll Never Do...."

I made two vows about dating: (1) that I would never lay one hand on a girl with sex on my mind until the day we were married and (2) that I would never tell a girl, "I love you" unless I could sincerely ask with my next breath, "Will you marry me?"

When I say that to an auditorium full of teenagers, I usually get all kinds of reactions. People gasp, drop their jaws, or laugh. But think about this for a minute: the words "I love you" have lost a lot of meaning, a lot of their permanence, in today's culture.

How often have you said (or imagined saying) "I love you" to someone of the opposite sex? Are you still in love with that person today? Probably not. Surveys show that the average person falls in love four times before meeting the person he or she eventually marries. That's why it is so important to never say those words until you mean it.

I had been dating my wife-to-be for four and a half months, and I had already told her parents that I wanted to marry her before I ever said, "I love you, Michelle." She flew into Dallas to see me. I picked her up in a red Coupe Deville Cadillac convertible. Man, I was a low-riding Chicano. I pulled up, jumped out, opened up her door, and she slid across those red leather seats. I walked back around to my side, got in, looked at her, and said, "Michelle, I love you. Will you marry me?" I leaned over and gave her a lip-lock that she hasn't forgotten to this good day! Then I reached in my pocket and pulled out a big piece of the rock. (Actually, it was more like a piece of the sand, but when you're in love it looks big.) When I said, "Michelle, I love you," she knew it really meant something.

Now guys, I need to tell you something. It was six l-o-n-g months until we were married. My wife is very good-looking, and every time I saw her I couldn't help but think about what was about to be *mine, all mine!* But I remembered my first commitment, and I never touched her sexually until the day we got married. After all these years she still says to me, "Jacob, I am more grateful than ever that we did everything right." Sometimes people ask me why that good-looking woman married me. I guess it is because God is good and love is blind. But the truth is, if I had not stuck to those two commitments, she probably would have dumped me.

Trust or Bust

When you wait until the right time, sex can cement your relationship together. But if you jump the gun, you plant a seed of mistrust that can follow you for many years to come. I've already mentioned this, but it is well-documented that teenage couples who were sexually involved before marriage trust each other less than those couples who waited for marriage. The reason is simple; before marriage, while they were dating, the guy says, "I just can't help myself." Finally, she gives in and he *helps himself.* You know that old memories don't go away very easily, especially the memory of the first time you have sex. After being married several years, when her husband is off on a business trip, what is her most vivid memory about him? It is that he can't help himself. If my marriage partner jumped the fence to be involved with me, what will keep him or her from jumping the fence again with someone else?

I travel a lot. I am in a different city and state twice a week. How does my wife know that she can trust me? How does my wife know that when I'm checking into some motel, some girl behind the counter isn't going to be checking me out? There are desperate women, you know. How does she know that some woman is not going to look at me and say, "Need some company, you tall, dark Mexican?" How does she know I won't be weak and give in? Girls, do you know how she knows? It's because when we were dating and even engaged, I never touched her improperly. I love her more today then I ever have before, so why would I touch someone that I don't even know or care about?

Guys, you may say, "But we're going to get married." True, you may get married, but most women relate sex to their first sexual experience. If her first sexual experience with you is filled with fear and guilt, it'll be hard for her to keep that out of her mind whenever she has sex after you're married. There is always that memory of guilt or even the feeling of being violated. Don't ruin the beauty and freedom of sex in your marriage by jumping the gun and planting the seed of guilt and mistrust in your relationship.

In other words, if you want to have a good shot at a marriage that lasts forever, you'd better marry a faithful person. Remember, I'm not talking about someone who just goes to church and pays lip service to Jesus Christ. I mean a guy or girl who has proven by his or her conduct with you to be faithful to Jesus Christ and concerned about what God says concerning sexual immorality.

Premarital sex plants the seed of all kinds of jealousy and mistrust. It's like building a house on sand. But if you set sexual guidelines from the beginning and stick to them, you'll build a relationship on a firm foundation and you won't plant any bad seeds. You see, I was planting trust in my marriage long before I was ever married. What are you planting in yours?

9 ▼ Returning to Virgin Territory

esearchers Masters and Johnson did a survey and found that religious women had the best sex lives of all the categories of women surveyed. I would guess that one of the reasons for this is that, as a group, they were much more likely to have saved sex until after they were married and that, therefore, they carried no guilt into the sexual relationship.

If a woman feels guilty because she gave in to her future husband, then the guilt is often followed by resentment. Ironically, the very thing they wanted in marriage—the freedom of sexual expression without guilt or shame—is the very thing they have lost. I've counseled with a lot of couples who were on the brink of divorce. I've discovered in those sessions that married couples who go ahead and have premarital sex lose respect for each other.

Facing the Inevitable Question

"Are you a virgin? Did you wait for me?"—the question is inevitable. Coming from the person you want to marry, those are nine powerful words. Some of you will drop your head, forced to say, "No, I didn't. I'm sorry." If you're a girl, there's no way you can hide the truth on your wedding night. And guys, don't even think about lying. She'll know it, or she'll find it out, and when she does, she'll probably never trust you again. As painful as it's going to be, you'd better prepare yourself, because she's going to want to know it all.

By now I'm sure you've asked the question in your own mind, *Jacob, were you a virgin on your wedding night?* My wife had waited for me, but when she asked me, I had to say, "No."

Hold on a second, some of you are saying to yourself. *Where does this guy get off telling me to do something he couldn't do himself? You had your fun, but you don't want us to have ours.*

There are a lot of single men and women who have made the decision to remain pure until they are married, people like A.C. Green, an all-star forward for the Phoenix Suns. A well-known player in the NBA gets more opportunities for sex in a week than most guys have in a lifetime. But when A.C. became a Christian at Oregon State University, he decided then and there to wait for his future wife. He's a great example.

But, no, I'm not an example like that. In the Mexican ghetto of Houston where I was raised, I had taken and sold drugs from the time I was nine until I was almost fifteen years old. My mother and father were going through many marriage relationships. I had four sisters who had all gotten pregnant or married by the age of sixteen. By the time I was thirteen years old I had done everything that you could do a number of times.

But when I was almost fifteen years old a man came to my school. He told me that Christ could change my life. I listened to him and did what he said. That man became like a father to me. He took me into his own home, and on most weekends I would live with him and his family. They raised me like their own son for eight years. He shared with me a principle called "second virginity." He told me that, even though I wasn't a virgin, I could start my second virginity.

I knew that one day I would be faced with the inevitable question. When my wife asked, "Jacob, are you a virgin? Did you wait for me?" this is what I said: "No, Michelle, I'm not. But I began my second virginity when I was almost fifteen years old, and from that day until our wedding day—nearly eight years later—I have never been with another girl. I've been waiting just for you."

Let me tell you, if there is anyone who was messed up and sexually spent, it was me. If there was anyone too dirty to get clean, it would have been me. I guess the people with whom I identify most are those who have blown it, not just once or twice, but completely, as I did. But because I started over and because I got rid of the guilt and shame, I know you can.

How to Get the Stains Out

In one college survey almost half of those questioned stated they were really sorry they had been involved in premarital sex. Almost 30 percent of those surveyed found it very difficult to forgive themselves. People try to deal with the guilt of their sin in various ways. Let me list a few.

TOP TEN WAYS TO TRY TO GET RID OF GUILT

Number 10: Congratulate yourself for minor acts of responsibility. *Hey, I practice safe sex.*

Number 9: Pray before committing fornication. *Now I lay her down to bed, ignoring what your Word has said....*

Number 8: Blame it on Satan. *Oops, the devil made me do it.*

Number 7: Blame it on God. *If God didn't want me to have sex with all those people, then he should have made me stop.*

Number 6: Blame it on other people. *I was seduced every single time!*

Number 5: Convince yourself that what you did wasn't really sin. *Perhaps God really meant for it to be the "Ten Suggestions."*

Number 4: Try to balance out the bad with the good. *Join the Peace Corps and feel better about yourself.*

Number 3: Go to church. *Those attendance pins must be good for something.*

Number 2: Compare yourself to some really bad people. *Hey, I'm better than the average, and surely God grades on a curve. I mean—I'm not Madonna. Look at Jeffery Dahmer. There are a lot of people worse than me.*

And the **Number 1** way people try to rid themselves of guilt: *I PROMISE—I'LL NEVER DO IT AGAIN!!*

How to Make All Things New

If you've blown it, today you can start your second virginity. You can start by receiving the gift of righteousness. As a result, you can know in your heart that in the eyes of God you are pure and clean. You need to see yourself as a gift that God is going to give to the person with whom you are going to spend the rest of your life. Begin saving yourself right now! Make a commitment today and draw firm guidelines. Save yourself for that special person. In God's timing, if and when you are married, God will say to you, "Go for it!"

Maybe you have been sexually abused or date-raped. I want you to know that as far as I'm concerned and as far as God is concerned *you're still a virgin!* Your virginity is something you give away, not something that you can have taken from you.

If you've never had to live with a heavy weight of guilt on your heart, you may not realize how hard it is to get rid of it. In fact, there's really only one way, and that one way is found in the gospel (or Good News) of Jesus Christ. The Bible tells us,

> Therefore, if anyone is in Christ, he is a new creation; old things have passed away; behold, all things have become new.
>
> 2 CORINTHIANS 5:17, NKJV

God just doesn't clean you up a little bit and put a bandage over your sin; he makes you a new creation. We also read:

> For as high as the heavens are above the earth, so great is his lovingkindness toward those who fear him. As far as the east is from the west, so far has he removed our transgressions (sins) from us.
>
> PSALMS 103:11-12

> "Come now, and let us reason together," says the Lord. "Though your sins are as scarlet, they will be as white as snow; though they are red like crimson, they will be like wool."
>
> ISAIAH 1:18

Now some of you may be thinking, *Jacob, you don't know what I've done and you don't know how guilty and dirty I feel.* I think I can understand very well how you feel, but even if I don't, I know that God delights in forgiving people, especially those who realize how much grace and mercy they need. Saul of Tarsus was the most fanatical persecutor of the early Christians. He chased them, spied on them, put them in jail, and even had some of them killed. Saul, who later changed his name to Paul, said of himself:

It is a trustworthy statement, deserving full acceptance, that Christ Jesus came into the world to save sinners, among whom I am foremost of all. And yet for this reason I found mercy, in order that in me as the foremost, Jesus Christ might demonstrate his perfect patience, as an example for those who would believe in him for eternal life.   1 TIMOTHY 1:15-16

The Apostle Paul was saying, in other words, that Jesus saved him, the worst sinner of all, to show the world that he could and would save *anybody*—even you.

Charlene is a contemporary example of God's grace. Here's what she had to say:

My dad died when I was twelve, and from that point on I was always trying to get guys to like me. When I first started dating in my early teens, the different guys were always trying to get me to go all the way, but I was scared. Eventually, when I was fifteen, one guy came along who was very forceful. He insisted we go to bed, and I couldn't resist him. From that time on I clung to him like a puppy dog. I was afraid no one else could ever care about me even though I knew he really didn't love me. I had some bad experiences with drugs and ended up running far away from home and from him.

In my new world I realized that I had become a woman and that I could use my sexuality to get whatever or whoever I wanted. I was really shocked to see this work. It was a real game to me.

Then one day I woke up and realized that nothing had any value to me. I had everything anyone could ever ask for, but it meant nothing to me. All my friends envied me, but I was miserable.

When I came to know Jesus Christ, my whole world changed. I finally understood how sinful I'd been and how precious sex is in God's sight. I was so ashamed that I had been used like a toy. But God miraculously gave me a husband who loves him. We have both had immoral pasts, but God has made us feel clean and new again. If he did that for me, I know he can for you, too.

God forgives and justifies people, that is, he makes them just as if they had never sinned. But God doesn't forgive or *erase* sin for no reason. He forgives on the basis of the penalty for sin having been paid in full. The lifeblood of his Son, Jesus Christ, was an atoning sacrifice for your sin and for the sin of the whole world. God forgives your sin because—and only because—it was done away with on the cross. Consequently, forgiveness and righteousness are given freely to all those who will receive it.

Here's how you receive.

1. Confess your sin. It's not like you're telling God something he doesn't already know. He saw what you did each time. It doesn't necessarily mean you have to remember and confess every single sin you have ever committed. For some of you that could be a pretty long prayer. What you should confess, or rather acknowledge, is essentially this: that you are a sinner and that your sin has separated you from God. God knows that. He's just been waiting for you to admit it. Secondly, you must acknowledge that it is *only* by the blood of Jesus Christ, not your own efforts, that your sins can be forgiven.

> If we say that we have no sin, we are deceiving ourselves, and the truth is not in us. If we confess our sins, he is faithful and righteous to forgive us our sins and to cleanse us from all unrighteousness. 1 JOHN 1:8-9

2. Repent of your sins. To repent means to turn around and go in another direction. It's more than laying off premarital sex. It means that you see the way you have lived, you hate it, and you turn away from it. Repentance means that you stop serving self and acknowledge Jesus Christ as the Lord of your life. That's real repentance.

> If you confess with your mouth Jesus as Lord, and believe in your heart that God raised him from the dead, you shall be saved; for with the heart man believes, resulting in righteousness. ROMANS 10:9-10, NAB

3. Receive the gift of righteousness by faith. I heard a pastor tell a story recently about a woman in his church. Every time a call was given for people who needed prayer, she would step forward and come weeping to the front. This scene would recur at almost every service.

Finally, the pastor asked her, "Why do you come up week after week?" The woman answered with her head down, "Twenty years ago my husband and I were involved sexually before we were married, and I've never been able to forgive myself." (So often it is the woman who suffers most with guilt. A life of guilt is a high price to pay for one night of pleasure.) The woman was sorry and even repentant, but being sorry, changing her behavior, walking down the aisle of the church, and even crying and begging did not earn her forgiveness.

The righteousness of God bought for us on the cross is received by faith. It is an *act of faith* in which we accept what he has done for us.

You may be a person who has come to the point at which you are ready to give your life to Jesus Christ, to accept him as your Lord and Savior, and to receive the forgiveness and cleansing he purchased for you on the cross. You do that by sincerely praying something like this:

God, I come to you in the name of Jesus acknowledging that I am a sinner, separated from you because of the things I have done. Today I want to repent of my sins, and I want Jesus Christ to be the Lord of my life from this day onward. I acknowledge that there is no amount of good works or anything I could offer to earn or deserve the gift of salvation and forgiveness. But I put the whole weight of my trust in Jesus Christ alone for my salvation. By faith in what he has done on the cross, I receive now the gift of forgiveness and righteousness, and I receive the Holy Spirit into my heart. Thank you, Father.

Cuttin' Loose from the Past

There are two things that happen when we become a Christian. He forgives what we have done, and he changes who we are. Another way of putting it is this: he removes the penalty of sin through his forgiveness, and he delivers us from the power of sin that has kept us in bondage. As we grow stronger in the Lord, we become more assured of God's forgiveness and more free from sin because of the power of his presence living within us.

Getting free from sin involves breaking free from our past sinful ways. Maybe for you there's going to be no other way than to make a clean and complete break with the person with whom you have been sexually involved. If that's what God's Spirit is saying to you, you'll know it very clearly in your heart. What you need to be careful about is letting the devil, your friends, or the person you've been going with talk you out of what you need to do. You need to listen to God and courageously follow his leading.

Besides getting free of current sinful relationships, you need to cut yourself loose from any ties to people from the past, even those with whom you are no longer associated. There are two things that keep us bound to the people of our past.

First of all, there is a bond created between two people when they have sex. "The two will become one flesh," the Bible says (1 Corinthians 6:16). In prayer, renounce all your ties with all former sexual partners. Declare your freedom from bondage. Ask the Holy Spirit to break any ties and set you free.

Second, we are bound to people and to past events by our lack of forgiveness for their offenses against us. This is going to be a tough one for some of you. It is so important that you forgive what others have done to you. You'll never get free from them if you don't. Bitterness, resentment, and unforgiveness allow what they did to you to keep on destroying your life.

I heard a story a few years ago about a woman who was kidnapped and raped repeatedly for three days. She was found and taken to the hospital. Eventually, she was examined by a psychologist who was probably a Christian because he dared to bring up the issue of forgiveness. It was a touchy subject. How could someone even suggest that a woman who had been treated that way simply forgive her attackers? To the psychologist's surprise, the woman said, "I have already forgiven them. They took me for three days. I will not give them any more."

Jesus taught a parable about a king and a man who owed him an enormous debt, equal to approximately ten million dollars in today's money. If the man did not pay, he and all his family would be sold as slaves. The man fell down before the king and begged for mercy. Consequently, the king actually forgave the entire amount.

This same man soon afterward went out and apprehended a man who owed him a single day's wages. He demanded payment and refused to show mercy. Pretty soon the king found out what was going on. Jesus concluded the story like this:

Then summoning him, his lord said to him, "You wicked slave, I forgave you all that debt because you entreated me. Should you not also have had mercy on your fellow-slave, even as I had mercy on you?" And his lord, moved with anger, handed him over to the torturers* until he should repay all that he owed him. So shall my heavenly Father also do to you, if each of you does not forgive his brother from your heart.

MATTHEW 18:32-35, NAB

The point Jesus was trying to make here is obvious. God forgave us of all of our sins, and certainly not because we deserved it. When we refuse to forgive others, it is as if we have forgotten or have taken lightly the grace and mercy of God extended to us.

Jesus also said:

Do not judge, or you too will be judged. For in the same way you judge others, you will be judged, and with the measure you use, it will be measured to you.   MATTHEW 7:1-2, NIV

In other words, the grace and mercy you extend to those who have hurt and transgressed against you is the same measure of grace that God will extend to you. Man, when I think about how much grace I have received and how much I'm going to need, I suddenly become very forgiving!

Reconciliation is a two-way street. Some of you may have been the stumbling block for others. The Holy Spirit may lead you to go back to some people and ask forgiveness. That could be very

---

*Torturers are things that torment us because of our unforgiveness like anger, fear, jealousy, and bitterness.

difficult in some situations and therefore easily put off. But listen to what Jesus said.

> If therefore you are presenting your offering at the altar, and there remember that your brother has something against you, leave your offering there before the altar, and go your way; first be reconciled to your brother, and then come and present your offering. MATTHEW 5:23-34

God has forgiven you and wants you to be free from your past. By forgiving those who have hurt you and asking the forgiveness of others, you loose yourself from the bondage of past sin.

Hanging on to Forgiveness

The Holy Spirit speaks to your heart and convicts you of your sin. But Satan and the demonic forces of hell also speak thoughts into your mind in order to turn you away from God, to prevent you from receiving his gift of righteousness.

Jesus said that the devil is the father of lies. Here's an example of how he lies to you. First he says, "It's OK to have premarital sex. Forget what the Bible and your conscience say. It'll be so much fun that you'll never regret it." That is Lie Number One.

Then after you fall into sexual immorality and realize that you have sinned against God, he says, "No, no; you're a very good person. You're not a sinner." That's Lie Number Two. The first lie gets you into sin. The second keeps you from receiving God's forgiveness because the first step to receiving grace is humbling yourself and admitting your sin.

After you admit your sin, repent and receive God's forgiveness, then comes the third lie. "You're such a *terrible sinner!* What makes you think God would ever forgive you?" That is Lie Number Three, also called the condemnation of the devil. After he tries to convince those who need the forgiveness of God that they don't need it, he tries to convince those who have received God's forgiveness that they are still guilty. The goal is always to keep you from growing in the Lord, to persuade you to give up and go back to the old way of living. The Apostle Paul wrote in his letter to the Romans:

> There is therefore now no condemnation for those who are in Christ Jesus. ROMANS 8:1

How can you tell the difference between the conviction of the Holy Spirit and the condemnation of the devil? Here are a few characteristics:

- *Conviction* of the Holy Spirit comes as a revelation of the heart of God. *Condemnation* is like an angry judge passing sentence.

- *Conviction* of the Holy Spirit is always very specific. "You have sinned because you did precisely *that,*" says the Holy Spirit. Satan's *condemnation* of a person is usually very general. "Well," he says, "it's not any one thing more than the other. You're just all messed up!"

- The goal of the Holy Spirit's *conviction* is to get you back into fellowship with God. "That thing you did was sin," he will point out. "Repent, receive forgiveness, and get back to walking with the Lord as quickly as you can!" The *condemnation* of the devil is always discouraging. "It's no use; you're just all messed up. You might as well quit! Go back to the way you were before. You haven't really changed."

It's not always easy to sort out the voices. But discernment definitely gets easier and easier as you (1) spend time each day reading the Bible, (2) spend time each day in prayer, and (3) begin to get together and build friendships with other Christians who are following the Lord. By doing these things faithfully, you grow in the Lord and in spiritual strength and maturity.

The Big Wedding Day

Throughout the New Testament, the church is referred to as the *Bride* of Christ, and the gathering of the saints after the second coming of Jesus Christ is called the *marriage* of the saints to the Lamb of God, Jesus Christ. The Apostle Paul writes in his letter to the Ephesian church:

> Husbands, love your wives, just as Christ also loved the church and gave himself up for her; that he might sanctify her, having cleansed her by the washing of water with the word, that he might present to himself the church in all her glory, having no spot or wrinkle or any such thing; but that she should be holy and blameless.   EPHESIANS 5:25-27

You see, the whole institution of marriage is a symbol of the relationship of Christ to the church (the entire number of Christians throughout the ages). Your own marriage is to symbolize this to the whole world: a bride and groom who have set themselves apart and kept themselves completely for one another. That is God's desire and purpose for you. Don't trade it for a cheap thrill. Don't let the devil or anyone else rip you off of God's best.

▼ Notes

ONE
Legends of Hot Love

1. James Patterson and Peter Kim, *The Day America Told the Truth* (New York: Prentice Hall, 1991), 45.
2. As quoted in *Research for Communicators* (Julian, Calif.: Josh McDowell Ministries).

TWO
Good Needs, Bad Deeds

1. Patterson and Kim, 66.

FOUR
The Grim Reaper of Great Relationships

1. Tim Timmons and Charlie Hedges, *Call It Love Or Call It Quits* (Fort Worth, Tex.: Worthy, 1988), 40.
2. *Sexual Health Update* (Austin, Tex.: Medical Institute for Sexual Health), April 1994, Vol. 2, No. 2.
3. As quoted by Josh McDowell at an AIDS briefing in Washington, D.C., February 1992.

$\mathscr{A}$ ring to help you say, "I don't"

BEFORE you say,

"$\mathscr{I}$ do."

The Rugged Cross™
for Boys

The Unblossomed Rose™
for Girls

True Love™
styles for Girls and Boys

The Gift Wrapped Heart™
for Girls

CHASTITY RINGS™
Prices begin at $45.

$\mathscr{H}$undreds of thousands of teens across America have made a solemn promise to God, and to themselves; to remain sexually pure until marriage.

No guilt. No disease. Just a life filled with promise.

Many wear a beautiful symbol of their promise–A Chastity Ring™, to remind them–at every moment–of the importance of their promise, and of the One who will help them keep it.

Just think–a ring to help you say, "I don't."

It will make you cherish all the more that other ring you will one day wear when you finally say, "I do."

Just show this ad to your favorite jeweler. For a free, color brochure, and the name of the jeweler nearest you, call (800) 668-9681, M-F, 8:00 AM to 7:00PM CST. Or write to: Chastity Rings, P.O. Box 53794, Lafayette, LA 70505.